Mom

I . . .

two better role
models . . . when it
comes to parenting!

DAD@HOME

I learned from
the BEST!

I hope I can
be half the <u>parent</u>!
that you were and
ARE to me!

Enjoy the book!

Love Greg

DAD@HOME

FULLY DOMESTICATED

By Gregory J. Tysowski

Dad@Home: Fully Domesticated
© 2016 Gregory J. Tysowski

ISBN-13: 978-0995828506
ISBN-10: 0995828504

First Edition, 2016

Printed in the United States of America

DEDICATION

*This is actually the hardest thing to write, as how
can I adequately put into words just how important
my wife and kids are to me? I must try.*

*They are my life, my hopes, my dreams
and my inspiration. They are my everything.
They are also my full-time job.*

This book is dedicated to Lianne, Abby and Daniel.

Your story is my story.

* *

ACKNOWLEDGEMENTS

This book needed a lot of support along the way and would not have been possible without a team of publishing industry professionals who helped transform a very rough first draft into a polished final product. Special thanks go out to my agent, Anne Bougie-Johnson at Sparks Literary Consultants for providing me with such a thorough and enlightening manuscript evaluation. Your suggestions and notes made Dad@Home much stronger and your one-year effort of trying to secure a book deal will always be appreciated. I'd also like to acknowledge the services of Michèle Young at Eagle Eye Editing and Proofreading for revealing just how terrible my spelling and grammar actually are. Job well done. And last but not least, I'd like to give a shout out to Graphic Designer Melina Cusano for a truly wonderful cover design and book layout.

★ ★ ★ ★ ★ ★ ★ ★ ★ ★ ★ ★ ★ ★ ★ ★ ★ ★

CHAPTERS

SHE WAS SUPPOSED
TO WAIT FOR ME

I burst through our front door feeling moist and a little sticky. It was only late June, but it was easily the hottest day of the year. I had just come home from a rather sweltering Saturday round of golf, looking rather disheveled with my sweat-stained, wrinkled polo shirt and scruffy unshaven face. When I had left the house early that morning, we had agreed that Lianne and I would witness the results of our first-ever home pregnancy test together. Normally, I would simply enter our home like a normal person. On this day, I resembled Kramer crashing through Jerry's apartment door.

After breathlessly skidding into our foyer, I immediately knew our agreement was null and void. Firstly, Lianne must have been actively scanning the area for my arrival as she was already waiting for me just inside the front door. Secondly, she was sporting a cute but wry smile, and last but certainly not least … she was glowing. On any other day, I could have described Lianne as a tad "dewy" from heat, but I've come to learn that someone in her condition is best described as glowing. It was surreal, exciting, stomach churning and joyous, all tightly wrapped up in a ball of nervous energy. We hugged, then hugged again and then we were oddly silent for a moment. There was now a baby in our future, and our lives would never be the same.

"Take the test again!" I demanded, partially ruining that shared precious moment in time. This completely irrational request wasn't based on the need to verify the initial results, and it certainly wasn't because I didn't believe my wife when she told me she was pregnant with our first child. I just wanted to see for myself when the little plus sign on the test "stick" slowly turned pink. Damn it, I wanted to see it! After a quick eye roll, we headed to the bathroom. She obliged.

She was supposed to wait for me.

THE DECISION

Lianne peeing on a stick for a second time in one morning had once again confirmed that our little side project to increase the world's population by at least one human was well on its way to fruition. To be honest, for most of our almost seven years of marriage, the idea of having kids wasn't really on our radar.

Lianne and I were too busy enjoying the life we now wistfully look back on. There were dinners at nice restaurants and lunches on patios. Living a few blocks away from the movie theatre meant we saw almost every film worth seeing, year after year. We both love to travel, and we took full advantage of our childless status to see the world. Trips to Hawaii, Italy, Spain, Scotland and Indonesia were highlights of our early-married life. And the sleep! My God, do I remember those glorious weekends of sweet, sweet slumber.

Why would anyone mess with that? We had a good racket going, and I remember warning my parents that we could end up being one of those couples who decided never to have kids. So, what changed? Why did we decide to abandon this near utopian lifestyle?

The year was 2001, and we were both firmly entrenched in our early 30s, but only one of us was endowed with a ticking biological timepiece. There was a growing feeling that Lianne only had a relatively small window for ripe baby-making conditions, so we started having discussions about if we should do it, why we should do it and when we should do it. I figured we likely had the how and where parts covered.

A huge consideration was Lianne's feelings of guilt over having a career that sometimes had horrendously long hours, then having a child who would ultimately compete for quality time with a demanding and sometimes unforgiving profession. While the times are slowing changing, the busy, breadwinning father usually doesn't get tagged with the "absentee parent" label. That special designation is reserved for the mother who works long hours.

We actually both had jobs that could be crazy busy, and the thought of raising a newborn in that environment was rather daunting for both of us. Logistically, there were many questions about what would happen after Lianne took her maternity leave. The idea of both of us working our deadline-laden jobs while fighting over which one of us would try to pick up the baby from a day home at 5:00 p.m. seemed out of the question. I recall overhearing this very animated debate several afternoons each week in an office down the hall from mine. Who was going to raise this kid?

Was a nanny the answer? We knew a few families that had live-in help and, while we could afford the expense, we weren't sold on the idea of someone who wasn't family being the primary caregiver of our child. Not that there's anything wrong with that! I always say, to each his own, and each family has to do what is best for their situation. I've seen firsthand how a nanny can truly become a part of the family, but we simply didn't think it would suit our lifestyle. And, to be honest, our home just didn't have enough room to accommodate another adult human being living in it. It was designed for a family of four – tops, and right from the get-go, that was the only number of family members we had in mind.

The final solution stemmed from evaluating our respective job situations.

Lianne had just been made partner at her law firm, and I had been working in the advertising department of the country's biggest sporting goods company. Lianne's annual income completely dwarfed mine and, while I liked my job and the people I worked with, it was my willingness to entertain the idea of becoming a stay-at-home dad that really sealed the deal and solved our biggest post-delivery problem.

I studied journalism in university, worked in television broadcasting for a few years, and endured the weird shift work that came with it. After a couple of years of rarely seeing my new bride, I switched gears and took a job in advertising to experience a regular Monday-to-Friday workweek. I missed the news gathering biz, but having a life trumped any misgivings I may have had about leaving it. Lianne and I truly enjoyed spending our evenings and weekends as a couple once again. Starting at the bottom rung in my department, my new job was fast-paced and stressful at times, but I liked learning about a new field and enjoyed a fun workspace.

As a lawyer in a large firm, Lianne would always be the main breadwinner of our family. There was nothing short of me cooking meth that would garner a salary that could even come close to hers. So, after a few years of working in advertising and even being promoted a couple of times, I decided that continuing my relatively low-paying career just wasn't enough for me to put the brakes on our grand plan to expand our operation. I was going to exit the workforce and enter the homefront. Now, all we had to do was get pregnant.

NINE MONTHS OF HEAVEN, NINE MONTHS OF... WELL, NOT SO MUCH

My wife is nothing if not thorough. Before we even started the process in the fall of 2001, Lianne was already buying books, doing the research, and making sure we had all of our ducks in a row before we got this party started. I, on the other hand, was simply chomping at the bit to do my part – eager to sire an heir to the Tysowski Empire. I had the easy job, and I predicted that knocking up my wife was going to be a snap.

It wasn't. Who knew that going off the pill after several years of use could really mess up the natural order of a woman's reproductive system? I certainly didn't know this little tidbit of information, but I do know one thing. Dragging out the baby-making process may have started to become a chore for Lianne, but I always chose to see the silver lining.

Lianne was routinely taking her temperature and charting her ovulation to determine the best possible time to conceive. There were times when I was ordered to get to work, and I happily obliged. We had a system and, by God, it was going to work. But, as the weeks turned into months, I got the feeling that Lianne was feeling rather discouraged with the process. When we found out that most doctors usually won't even bat an eye until you've been trying to get pregnant for the better part of a year, it seemed like we could be in this for the long haul. The regimen continued, along with the charting and the information gathering.

We had to increase our odds of conceiving, and it was determined that between periods of ovulation it was recommended that I keep up my sperm count by engaging in regular intimate coupling sessions. Again, I was more than happy to do my part, as it was apparent that Lianne had little to no idea that I was routinely and frequently accomplishing this feat as a solo act. So, as more weeks of trying to put a bun in the oven morphed into months, I found myself with a spring in my step and more action than I've had since our honeymoon.

I am fully aware of the irony that comes with using that analogy, as we all know what happens to honeymoons. Sure enough, in June of 2002,

Lianne was late with her period and we headed to Shoppers Drug Mart to buy our inaugural home pregnancy kit. We were nervous and excited with what the results would show, and how it would change our lives in a heartbeat. Just having the test in our possession seemed crazy! The box sat on the bathroom countertop that evening, but we decided to wait until morning to take the test.

I was getting up super early for a sweaty Saturday round of golf, and Lianne had agreed to wait until I returned before taking it. You already know that an overwhelming surge of curiosity got the best of her, and I was greeted at the door with that cute but wry smile. We were officially prego, and my nine months of heaven would make way for Lianne's nine months of … well, not so much.

I don't profess to be an expert on the changes a woman goes through during the nine-month gestation period. But, from what I witnessed from my front row seat, I continue to be overjoyed to this day that I never had to do any of the heavy lifting. My contribution to the miracle of new life was a simple seed. Lianne had to manufacture, transport and deliver that precious cargo.

The first signs of trouble are the morning sickness, and there was no shortage of that. It seemed like from the get-go, this whole "having a baby" thing sucked some serious ass for the person carrying the payload. The body also begins to change, and sometimes in ways that are pleasing to male sensibilities. However, the "you can look but don't touch" policy was instituted at an early stage in the pregnancy, and it found a significant foothold.

I must say that I could not complain or even think about complaining. I was still fresh off a great run, and now I understood the consequences of my nine-month tour of duty. Add to the mix a tired, sickly and grumpy wife and you've got yourself a recipe for a lengthy stretch of solo missions. Again, I must stress that my minor inconveniences that I experienced during this pregnancy marathon were a mere speck of dust in the vast universe of uncomfortable problems Lianne had to endure.

It seemed once the morning sickness passed, there would be a new set of aches, pains and hormones to contend with. By the later months, Lianne could rarely find a comfortable position to sleep, sit or breathe. I recall our bed suddenly becoming home to our very first threesome. It was made up of Lianne, me and our new bedfellow: a giant body pillow that I named Bruce. It seems Lianne's inability to have a good night's sleep in those last couple of months was simply Mother Nature's way of prepping pregnant women for the sleep deprivation they are about to experience once that bundle of joy pops out.

During the entire pregnancy, I was keen on going to the doctor's office for the regular prenatal tests and check-ups, and I was there for all but one of them. Words really can't explain how a dad-to-be feels when he first hears that tiny, hummingbird-fast heartbeat, or when he finally sees that first alien image on the ultrasound. Each one is a milestone that both excites and terrifies at an almost equal rate. We decided that we didn't want to know if it was a boy or a girl, as we thought that was still one of life's great and magnificent surprises. In retrospect, I'm so glad we didn't know, as the anticipation adds so much to the delivery experience.

By the grace of God, we had no health problems during the pregnancy, and I still remember our last check-up before Lianne's due date. The doctor was sure that she was ready to pop any day, and we were still several days before the actual due date. Would we have this baby early? As it turned out, our baby had a timetable and was sticking to it. Almost a week later than we expected, Lianne went into labour … a long, hard, never-endingly long, hard labour. Did I mention it was hard?

JUST TAKE THE DRUGS!

The date was March 22, 2003, and it had started out just like any other late pregnancy day for Lianne. Her belly-bump was exploding outward, yet somehow contained in that drum-tight, ever-stretching skin. To see her from behind, she looked like anyone else, but as she turned to expose that side profile, it was almost comical to see how 99 per cent of her weight gain was right there in that exercise ball of a gut.

Then it all started. The first contraction was in the early afternoon, and it didn't seem all that bad (according to my wife). It soon passed, and I already had my stopwatch out to see when the next one would arrive. I was hoping they would come fast and furious, as I wanted to get this show on the road. I wanted to go to the hospital! I wanted to meet our baby! It didn't work out quite that way.

Contractions were few and far between to start, and Lianne and I ended up taking a nice springtime walk in our neighbourhood to help pass the time and try and get those baby-delivering juices flowing. By the time we came home, I had put away my stopwatch as it became apparent that this was going to be a lengthy process. A few more hours passed, and the contractions started to come marginally faster. Surely, now was the time to pack up Lianne's little overnight bag and drive to the hospital.

The hospital was only a five-minute drive away, so we were there in no time at all. After parking and checking in, we waited patiently in the examination room, thinking Lianne would be admitted shortly and we would be on our way to the strange and wonderful new world of parenthood. We were justifiably deflated when the doctor took one look at Lianne's hoo-hah and gave us a two-word assessment: "Go home." Lianne had only dilated two centimetres, and that wasn't far enough along to keep her at the hospital. Not even close. So, we made the slow walk of shame out of the maternity ward, back to the parking lot and back to our house.

Contractions were still coming, but at a pretty slow clip so we decided that we should just wait it out and try sleeping. After a restless night, the next day started off as it had ended; but after a few more hours of increasing discomfort and more frequent contractions, we decided to head back to the hospital. We hoped against hope that we wouldn't get the boot again, and we were relieved when Lianne had progressed just enough to allow us to set up shop. Four centimetres wasn't exactly a long way down the path to delivery, but we avoided a second shame-filled walk and that was a small victory.

As we moved later into the evening, Lianne's contractions were getting more uncomfortable by the minute, but we weren't leaping forward in the process very quickly. Lianne's water hadn't even broken yet, so the doctor took care of that manually and predicted that would speed things along. It didn't, and the pain was starting to take its toll on Lianne, and to a much lesser extent … me.

To top things off, it was determined that Lianne was experiencing back labour, which meant the baby was positioned in a way that was absolutely killing Lianne's lower back.

During our pre-natal classes, it was obvious that our instructor was extremely pro "natural" childbirth. She would start off the discussion by taking great pains to explain that the decision whether or not to request an epidural was completely up to us. Then she would dive into a cautionary tale where a mom-to-be was fully dilated and ready to pop, and then completely derailed the process by demanding drugs! In the end, that "silly" woman needed a C-section when she was just minutes away from blissfully delivering her miracle baby drug-free. Our instructor would then reiterate that the decision was completely up to us, and that she wasn't trying to sway us. Yeah right, lady.

Her words must have resonated with both of us, as our informed decision was to go "au naturel" with the delivery. That well-intentioned plan started to unravel after a couple more hours of Lianne enduring increasingly painful back labour. Our nurse was eager to help and suggested that I could help Lianne's intense pain by pressing down on her tailbone while she had a hot shower. So into the shower she went, and there I was, trying to stay dry while only sticking my right arm into the shower stall. Lianne was slightly bent over, her naked bum facing me, while I pressed down on her tailbone with the palm of my hand. My entire torso was getting drenched by the splattering shower droplets, so after ten to fifteen minutes of this madness I yelled over the din of the spraying water, "Is this helping even a little bit?"

"NO!" Lianne bellowed back, "not at all! Nothing is helping!"

It seemed this shower experiment was an exercise in futility, so I yelled again, "I think you should just take the drugs!" I think Lianne may have been waiting for me to bring up the topic, like she inexplicably needed permission from me to ask for an epidural! I was witnessing my wife go through a painfully slow descent into delivery hell, and yet I could tell that a part of her still wanted to stick to the plan. I was thinking, "Screw the plan!" I'm not saying I convinced her to take the drugs, but I think it helped that I was all for it. This was definitely not what we signed up for, as the hours of excruciating contractions had sapped Lianne's strength and somehow mine as well.

The doctors set up the procedure, and my job was to help hold Lianne still while they inserted a lengthy needle directly into her spine. Damn it! Into her spine! By now the contractions were coming quicker, and it was paramount that Lianne lay perfectly static while the needle was going in. My jaw dropped when I saw the insertion and my only thought was, "Thank God Lianne isn't seeing this."

The relief from the pain was almost magical, for both of us. It allowed Lianne to get a few hours of much needed rest before the big push, and it also got me back on track and ready for the delivery.

After our nurse dimmed the lights, I pulled out the hide-a-bed couch in Lianne's hospital room and I immediately crashed. I know I won't get a whole lot of sympathy from women who have been through childbirth, but I was already completely wiped out by the process and likely fell asleep in about ten seconds.

The flickering of fluorescent lighting and the buzz of activity around Lianne's spread legs jarred me from my deep slumber. It was go time! I rubbed my eyes, put on a green scrub, and joined the conversation. She was fully dilated and the process of pushing out our first-born was finally given the green light. I was right at Lianne's side the whole time, doing whatever I could to help, but let's be honest for a moment. All the daddy really has to do is be a glorified cheerleader. The mommy is the real deal, and I could not have been prouder of Lianne as she sweated, grunted and pushed for over an hour.

I previously mentioned our attendance at a pre-natal course when discussing our decision to get the epidural. I think I can speak for Lianne when I say that those classes were an absolute waste of our time. Any breathing exercises or advice your instructor offers up is completely forgotten when you are right in the thick of it. The nurses have done this a million times, and they deserve major kudos for keeping us on track and telling Lianne exactly what she needed to do. In retrospect, there was one very useful bit of information that the pre-natal class provided to us.

During a tour of the delivery ward, we found out exactly where to go and who to talk to when first arriving at the hospital. That actually came in very handy, so I guess there's that.

Getting back to the story at hand, after more than thirty hours since Lianne's labour began, our baby made the grand entrance! I have to admit, I only took a single sneak peek at the action "down below" before rushing back to Lianne's side. That is a surreal sight that I won't soon forget, but I'm glad I saw it happen, if only for a few seconds.

We didn't want to know the sex of our baby, so we were both surprised and elated to finally meet our baby girl. I was offered the opportunity to cut the cord, and I took it. I was surprised at how thick the umbilical cord actually is and how tough it was to cut through that temporary tether to my wife. Another thing I was surprised with was the state of that delivery room! There were bloodied towels tossed around all willy-nilly, and then there was the splatter of the placenta delivery still fresh on the floor in front of Lianne's bed. It resembled a slaughterhouse, or perhaps a murder scene, and not a setting that showcases the miracle of new life ... but I digress.

By now it was 6:30 in the morning, but the excitement of the moment and the adrenaline rushing through my veins seemed to push aside any and all fatigue. After giving our daughter a thorough once over, the nurses wrapped her up and handed her over to Lianne. I was pleasantly surprised to see how cute she was, as most newborns that I've seen look a lot like Captain Jean-Luc Picard ... but not her. Not our Abigail Katherine Tysowski. She looked just like a sweet, little baby doll.

Looks can be deceiving.

THE COUNTDOWN

That first day with Abby was a busy one, filled with family visits, photos and generally good times. The nurse helped us give baby her very first bath, a lactation specialist was on hand to help with any breastfeeding questions, and then another doctor arrived to see how our bundle of joy was doing. Our little girl slept away most of the day, all wrapped up snug as a bug in rug. A sleeping baby is one of the sweetest sights you'll ever see, but it is generally a very short-lived phenomenon.

I decided that I wanted to spend the night at the hospital with Lianne and Abby. I had taken two weeks off work, and I wanted to do my part right off the bat. Unfortunately, there was no pull-out couch for me to crash on this time. Lianne was sharing a room with another new mom, and I was relegated to sleeping in a chair. As it turns out, it didn't really matter where I tried to sleep, as our sweet baby doll didn't want to sleep ... at all. I guess that's what happens when you sleep all day, but we never expected she would be this fussy from the very get-go.

Was she hungry? Try feeding her! She's not latching on! She won't stop crying! Why is she crying? Why won't she eat if she won't sleep? Why won't she sleep if she won't eat? I swear that first night lasted forever, and it only added to Lianne's (and my) sleep deprivation. Almost everyone who saw the first photos of me holding a newborn Abby in my arms says the same thing, "Greg, you look like shit!" In the good old days, the nurses took your baby away to some faraway location on the maternity ward, allowing the exhausted new mother to get some sleep. These days, your new addition to the family is rolled right in next to the bed, and every little squeak, squawk or whimper jolts you out of bed (or uncomfortable chair).

When morning arrived, we were told that the hospital was checking us out, a little over twenty four hours after Lianne was transferred out of the delivery room and into a recovery room. How's that for hospital efficiency? I had the base for the baby carrier already secured in the back seat; so all we had to do was strap little Abby into her car seat and head for home where our foray into the wonderful world of parenting would start for real.

As any new parent knows, those first few weeks can be torturous for the one with the boobs. Lianne started off her new occupation as mother with a thirty-hour labour and a terrible, sleep-deprived first night on the job. I mentioned earlier that I thank my lucky stars that I never had to do any of the heavy lifting during the pregnancy. I thank them again, a thousand times over that I didn't have to get up every two to three hours to feed a crying baby. The first few nights at home actually saw me get up with Lianne when she made her way into the nursery to pacify and nourish our newborn. I actually had very good intentions to try to keep my wife company, but after a few minutes I would roll up on the floor and fall back to sleep. Lianne told me not to bother coming with her if all I was going to do was snore on the floor, so I stopped and my grand gesture failed miserably.

As days turned into weeks, it became apparent that Abby was more than just a fussy baby. She was crying the majority of her waking hours, and there was nothing we could do about it. It was official. We had a colicky baby, and after my two-week stint at home, I went back to work to leave Lianne home alone to deal with it.

For those of your who don't know what I'm talking about is, here's a quick description from *MedicalNewsToday*. Colic is an attack of furious crying brought on by what appears to be abdominal pain and is estimated to affect up to 20% of babies in their first few months. The intense crying episodes cause babies faces to become red and flushed and can last a few minutes, to much longer periods. They seem to occur at the same time every day – generally during the late afternoon or early evening and can start suddenly and for no apparent reason.

That's the official description, and while fairly accurate, our experience was not limited to late afternoon or early evening. There were many teary phone calls to me at the office at all hours of the day with Abby crying in the background and Lianne crying in my ear. I felt terrible, but there wasn't much I could do except listen and show support. There were a couple of times when I had to cut one of Lianne's emotional phone calls short, citing an imaginary department-wide meeting that was starting in two minutes. I do feel a little bad about that, but I knew that the second I walked through the door back home I was immediately going to be handed our fussy-faced kid.

I remember us taking shifts wearing out a path in the carpet on the main floor of our house. Abby would calm down if you kept her moving, but the second you set her down or even tried to sit down with her still in your arms, the ear-splitting cry of the kraken would be released again. If you think that I'm exaggerating at how loud our baby was, then think again. We didn't use a baby monitor at night, as we had no use for it. That scream could be heard a mile away, let alone in the next room. From time to time, we would try venturing out into public, like joining my family for a nice dinner at a restaurant. Just like at home, we would have to take shifts walking Abby around the restaurant, but at least this time we had other family members pitching in and taking a turn.

Other babies behaving like "regular" infants always seemed like such a foreign concept. At the mall, I would see a little baby just sitting in his car seat next to his couch-sitting, coffee-sipping mother for what seemed like an eternity. That kid had his hands in his mouth, or some chewed up toy, and would just sit there. There was no infuriating tantrum set off by God knows what. He would just park himself, look around, and see the sights for an hour ... so quietly! No fuss, no muss. I would sometimes ask other parents how their baby could accomplish such a herculean feat and most seemed downright confused as to why I would even ask. Can't someone simply put a baby down without it screaming its head off? Apparently, most of the world can, just not us.

Now and then, we would talk about kids with a couple that actually had experienced a colicky baby, and there was an immediate connection.

"Wow, someone else who actually gets it!" One of Lianne's work friends explained to us how he and his wife both really wanted a huge family, but stopped after only two kids. It turns out they got back-to-back babies with colic, and living through that trying experience was more than enough to put the brakes on recreating the 70s sitcom *Eight is Enough*. We tried not to complain about it too much as nobody wanted to hear about it, and nobody could really relate anyway. Sometimes, I'd confide in my mother when the crying was really getting to us, but there was no real usable advice coming from her. It turned out her babies rarely cried; and if they did, she would just shower them with even more love. That way, they knew they were safe and secure and the crying would soon stop. I guess topping off your baby with extra love is never a bad thing, but in this particular case, my mom's advice wasn't the permanent solution we were desperately seeking.

We did try any and all "cures" that we researched, but nothing worked. We swaddled Abby nice and tight during a crying episode, we changed her feeding times, we changed her formula once Lianne stopped breastfeeding, we changed the shape of the bottle, we changed the size of the holes in the bottle teats. No luck. It seemed hopeless at times.

I don't want to give the impression that living with our baby girl was a complete and utter nightmare 24/7, because it most certainly was not. There were some very sweet moments, like when she first woke up in the morning. Abby would smile, coo and lay on her back for fifteen to twenty minutes as Lianne changed her and clothed her for the day. Then something would change, and she would flip a switch and be endlessly fussy. Another reprieve was at bath time at the end of the day. Lianne and I would bathe Abby on the kitchen counter in this large white plastic baby tub. She seemed to really enjoy the warm water and being wrapped up all snuggly in a fluffy towel. It became a happy nightly tradition … happy until one night when we were entertaining a house full of family and friends.

We had just finished dinner and decided to give Abby her bedtime bath before putting her down for the night. Lianne suggested that we move the process upstairs, as there was too much hubbub on the main floor. I dismissed that crazy request and started the bath. Good Lord, I don't know what brought it on, but Abby started her banshee scream and didn't let up until we finished the bath and ran her up the stairs to her room. For almost fifteen minutes, all conversation stopped as every one of our guests slowly turned towards two very red-faced parents and a very unhappy infant. "I can't believe she can be that loud!" was uttered more than once.

This wasn't the first or last time our little bundle of volume shattered a pleasant ambiance and brought everyone's full attention on her. Lianne had a group of friends she called the "mommy group." It was a bunch of women with similarly-aged babies, and they would meet up and go for long walks with their respective strollers. Five babies, and only one of them would usually be screaming her head off. Just to be clear, I'm not saying that other parents never have to contend with crying babies. Obviously, every infant on planet Earth will cry or get very fussy when they need to be fed, changed, or put down for a nap. There are other reasons why babies cry that I'm glossing over, but I'm just trying to make it clear that we had a girl that wanted to bawl and bellow to her full lung capacity most of the day.

So, this is what we had to deal with during those precious first few months of parenthood. I had it so much easier being at the office until dinnertime, and I must admit that the prospect of me taking over after six months and becoming a permanent stay-at-home dad was becoming much less appealing as our baby continued to cry, cry, and cry. Lianne certainly got short-changed, as she wasn't eligible for the full one-year maternity leave that most women were now taking advantage of. My wife was now a partner, and no longer an employee. She was actually a trailblazer, being the first woman partner at her law firm to get pregnant. All of the other female partners had kids before being offered a spot in the partnership. She negotiated six months off work, and the grand plan was for me to take a six-month parental leave, and then never go back to my advertising job.

By now, baby Abby was over five months old and I had less than a month left of work before I made my major career change. The countdown had begun.

I WOULD BE WASHING THE DISHES

With only a few weeks of paid employment left, I found myself lying my ass off to almost every person in my department. "Don't you worry, I'll be back in six months! Don't let the place fall apart without me! Ha, ha," I would jest. Only a couple of my closest work friends knew the truth, and they promised to keep their big yaps shut. It turns out that I was also a bit of a trailblazer, as I was the first man to take a parental leave at my company. I would also be the first to quit his job right after making that very minor bit of history.

While I had made up my mind to become a full-time dad, there were a couple of wrinkles that made me pause and think twice, if only for a moment. Almost five years prior to my impending departure, I started a bottom rung job as a way to escape the late news nightshift, and have a more traditional nine-to-five lifestyle that I could share with my wife. However, a funny thing happened along the way. I had been promoted a couple of times, and just before I was leaving for my six month leave, the VP of Marketing told me that I would have another promotion waiting for me when I came back. At that time, I was the Account Manager for one of the smaller sporting goods chains that the company owned, and I was in charge of managing a $3,000,000 advertising budget. As far as my boss knew, I would be taking charge of the "big store" when I got back. That would mean a tidy pay hike and being entrusted with managing an ad budget of over $40,000,000. It was kind of a big deal.

If that wasn't enough, then came the word that my company had almost completed the construction of a new daycare right in the office. Throw in the still colicky baby girl who was waiting for me to take over her primary care duties, and I was starting to wonder if I was making a mistake. Lianne and I discussed the whole situation again, and despite the office daycare and opportunity for career advancement, the bottom line hadn't changed. If I stayed, we would both be working the same crazy, stressful jobs and the only one who would really suffer would be Abby. All the problems that a two-income family would face trying to raise a baby would still be there. Who would get home first and start dinner? Who would take Abby to her doctor's appointments? Who does the dishes? Another thing that hadn't changed was our financial situation. Pay increase or no pay increase, I was still making a small pittance compared to Lianne. We could definitely make it on one income, so it was settled. I would be washing the dishes.

I was glad that we had another discussion to clear the air, as it reaffirmed my decision to stay at home, and actually put my mind at ease as my countdown to stay-at-home fatherhood continued. The only substantial task that I had to accomplish before I packed it in was to hire a new production assistant to assist my old production assistant ... who was being promoted to take over my job. I interviewed several worthy candidates, and on my last day on the job, I gave the best of the bunch a job offer, which she accepted. All that was left to do was to attend a nice "going away" lunch put on by my advertising department buddies and go home.

I was relieved to conclude the hiring process, as my boss warned me that I was cutting it a little too close for comfort. My relief was short-lived. As it turned out, I wasn't done with work stuff just yet. Every time I think I'm out, they pull me back in.

On my first official day at home, I got a call from the office. My new hire had changed her mind and was taking another job offer. I didn't really have a back-up plan, and I recall making a flurry of calls with baby Abby in one hand, and a phone in the other. In the end, I was satisfied with my second choice and she ended up working out just fine. My mini-work crisis had temporarily sidetracked my attention from the momentous occasion of starting my new job. For two days, it had prevented me from really thinking about how my daily existence was about to change forever. Then it finally sunk in ... this was it. This was my new life.

A KEPT MAN

We had researched a fair bit about colicky babies and learned that it typically passes by the three-to-four-month mark. Abby finally did something typical and began to shed her whiney ways a couple of months before I took the reins. This was great news for me, and just another reason why Lianne got the short end of the stick. Her half-year shift at home was beyond frustrating. And, with a high-stress job, she was hoping for some happy fun times with our bouncing baby. While there were a few shining moments, my wife re-turned to her law firm wishing her time at home would have been much more rewarding and sim-ply more fun. If she had been eligible for a year-long maternity leave, she would have seen the incredible growth of our little girl. While some people love the helpless lump that is a newborn baby, I say they only get interesting after they can hold their heads up, sit on their own and start to explore their environment.

I had officially begun my tenure as chief domestic engineer, and I had to admit that it was not nearly as daunting as I had imagined. By now, Abby was on a fairly regimented schedule of napping, feeding and free time. Throw in six or seven diaper changes, and you've got yourself a pretty full day that seemed to go by very quickly. Sometimes, I'd chat up strangers that I'd meet on my daily errands. They'd see me with Abby in my arms or in the stroller and ask if I "had the day off" or if I was filling in for mommy today. When I explained that I was a stay-at-home dad, I would get plenty of reactions and comments, nearly every one of them overwhelmingly positive.

Sometimes people would go a little too far with their praise of my bold career choice proclaiming, "Oh you've got the toughest job of all … that's nothing to be ashamed of!" Some folks would go out of their way to prove to me just how OK they were with me being a stay-at-home dad, while others would act like they were trying to make me feel better, and convince me that I made a good decision: "You may not be sure about it now, but trust me, you won't regret this!" I would usually just smile and make some lame joke about still getting the hang of being Mr. Mom.

The most varied responses came from men. Without a doubt, the most common thing guys would usually say was:

"Man, I would love it if I could stay home with the kids! That's great."

I found that I would also get unsolicited advice from men who were not stay-at-home dads, but somehow had it all figured out. One weekend golf outing saw me paired up with a younger guy, a self-described "golf nut", who explained to me that he wasn't married, and didn't have kids. However, he had some thoughts about my situation and was positive that I could easily bring my one-year-old daughter to the driving range every day:

"Just think about how you could really sharpen up those approach shots if you worked on it every day!"

I responded with a half-hearted, "Um... yeah, I should try that next week", but in my head I was screaming:

"That's just about the stupidest thing I've ever heard in my life! Yup, I'm just gonna bring my wobbly-walking little toddler to a driving range! Hey, the club head speed when I swing my driver is only a hundred miles an hour, and there's no way fifty guys hitting projectiles all around me could be considered dangerous place for my baby!"

While that little gem of stellar parenting advice immediately fell on deaf ears, a scruffy-looking stranger who I met heading into the mall also had all of the answers. We struck up a conversation, and when he found out I was a stay-at-home dad, he was very excited to share an elaborate scheme he described as "pure genius", and told me that I would be a fool not to try it.

"All you have to do is find four other guys who are stay-at-home dads. It doesn't matter who they are or how you find them. Maybe you put an ad in the paper, that part doesn't matter. Here's what does matter – you all agree to take ALL of the kids in this little group just one day of the week. Sure, that one day of the week will be an insane experience, but you just have to survive it! Then you've got the other four days of the week to do whatever the hell you want. Just think about that, one day of hell for four days of freedom. Like I said, it's pure genius!"

I laughed it off with a "Hey, I really like that plan!", thanked the guy for the advice, and kept my stroller moving towards the mall entrance. I had to admit, in theory, that bat-shit crazy arrangement could actually work, but there are a lot of things in life that may work – in theory. In reality, that wasn't not sustainable child-care model, and if it really was such a great idea, wouldn't it be commonplace? Wouldn't smart stay-at-home moms also start up these "work one day a week" clubs?

It occurred to me that both of these well-intentioned strangers seemed to think there had to be a way us stay-at-home dads could somehow scam the system. Guys, I'm sorry, but you actually have to do the work. There are no shortcuts. And that's why plenty of other men would tell me they could never pull it off in a million years:

"I don't know how you do it! I would be so useless at this baby stuff."

The truth is, any guy could do what I do. Not knowing how to do something is really no excuse. You just have to want to do it. As the old saying goes, it ain't rocket science. Here's another cliché than is also true: if I can do it, anyone can do it.

The problem that many men have is the prospect of being relegated to a strictly child-rearing role and losing their traditional position as provider. I knew a two-income couple that had young kids at home, with the wife earning more than the husband. They struggled at times with balancing work and child-care and often had difficulty getting one of them to meet that 5:00 deadline at the day home. I asked her once if her husband ever considered staying at home and letting her bring home all of the bacon. She told me that she had hoped he would consider trying it, but the answer was always an unequivocal no.

He simply felt that he needed to contribute monetarily and just couldn't see himself as completely reliant on his wife for the family's financial security. I never thought of him as old-fashioned or slightly chauvinistic in any way. In fact, he seemed very much like a modern man, hip with the changing gender roles in our society.

He obviously wasn't, and I've come to learn that the overwhelming need to be a provider is a trait that is still very common in a majority of men I've met or interacted with. Another thing I've discovered is that it isn't just the obvious, testosterone-filled, macho man who would scoff at the idea of being a stay-at-home dad. It's actually the norm, and it's the reason why you still don't see that many of us out there. According to numbers released by Stats Canada, in 1976 only 2% of men identified themselves as a stay-at-home dad. Today, that number has jumped all the way up to 12%, and while that sounds like a seismic shift in gender and family dynamics, a lot of it has to do with economics. A major spike was noted in 2010, after the recession hit male-dominated industries far more than female. But even with the number of stay-at-home dads tripling in the past thirty years, that still leaves less than 60,000 of us across the entire country. As a group, we are hardly mainstream, but if there is one stat that is encouraging, it's this. Thirty years ago, only one in every 100 stay-at-home parents were dads. Today, it's one in eight.

The United States has witnessed an even more dramatic increase in the percentage of stay-at-home dads. Since 1989, the number has nearly doubled, from 1.1 million to almost 2.2 million but like Canada, much of the recent surge can be attributed to the lengthy recession that began in 2008. According to a Pew Research Center analysis of 2014 U.S. Census Bureau data, 16% of American households have a father staying home to take care of children and household duties. But almost a quarter of them are doing it only because they cannot find a job. Only 21% of the over two million American men staying home say the main reason is to care for their home or family. Compare that to the 73% of American women who report that they are home specifically to care for their home and family and the picture I'm painting becomes crystal clear.

Sure, there are more and more of us out there, but for many, the decision to stay home still comes down to necessity over nurturing. I actually chose this life, while many guys have their new role thrust upon them by external factors that are completely out of their control. It doesn't help that many men still face a stigma when they stay home to nurture their kids. A 2013 Pew survey found that only 8% or respondents said children are better off if their father is home without a job.

Anyone who knows me can tell you that I've never been some kind of "man's man" or tough guy, or hyper-masculine ... or whatever you call that kind of guy these days. That's not to say that I didn't have some reservations about having my yearly income drop to zero dollars and zero cents. I've mentioned before that my salary never came close to Lianne's, but in my head I would calculate that my meager monthly wage still paid the mortgage and some other household bills. It wasn't that much, but at least it was something. My income actually made a difference, and now it was all gone. I was now a kept man, as some people liked to joke.

Did it bug me? Did I feel like less of a man? Did I experience feelings of inferiority, a loss of self-esteem or self-respect? Fortunately, I did not and I'll tell you why. I knew in my heart and soul that what I was doing was important ... way more important than earning a paycheque or succeeding at any job I've ever had or will have. That being said, I've never worn my role as a stay-at-home dad like some badge of honour. I don't advertise it, or blurt it out to strangers every chance I get. Rather, I'll let other people ask what I do and will happily talk about it with anyone who inquires. It's a weird situation to be in, as I'm definitely not ashamed of my role in our family, but I'm not shouting from the rooftops about how happy I am with my job either. Think of it this way; how many little boys dream of being a househusband when they grow up? It's not something most people see as a life choice when they are younger, but, like I said before, what I do is essential and with each passing year I'm seeing exactly how I've helped shape our family's path.

I've been asked before if I ever felt like I was "taking one for the team," and that made me think. At first, I thought that maybe I did feel like that sometimes, but then I would stop and really contemplate that query. I don't think anyone would ask a woman that question, as society views child rearing as primarily the mother's responsibility. How can taking care of your kids be considered taking one for the team? The question suggests that a domestic life of raising children and maintaining a household is somehow beneath a man, or some kind of unjust sacrifice, and I can tell you that it is neither. What it is … is complicated, and by the end of this book I hope I can make some sense of it all and in the process, give you some appreciation of what it's like to have my job.

One of the ways I can explain what it is to be a stay-at-home dad is to divulge some of the many conversations and reactions that I've had with people who find out what I do.

BUT AREN'T YOU SO BORED?

Every week, Abby and I would attend a music class called "Baby and Me." There, I would sit in a circle with seven moms bouncing our kids on our laps, playing instruments and singing songs. It was a nice way to familiarize our tiny offspring to the wonders of new sounds, rhythm and percussion. We had to introduce ourselves at the start of the year, so they all knew I was a stay-at-home dad and nothing more was ever said about it. No big deal.

That changed one week when a grandma had to fill in for one of the moms in our little music circle and she approached me after class ended.

"Oh how precious", the grandmother said, making peek-a-boo faces at Abby in the car seat. Shifting her grandson on her hip, she then asked me, "Are you filling in for Mommy too?"

"Nope," I said with a forced smile, "this is my full-time day job."

Her jaw dropped... "Really?" Her eyes widened, then after a few more seconds she added, "Well do you cook, too?"

"I'm not exactly a wizard in the kitchen," I replied, "but it's my job to make sure there's food on the table when my wife comes home from work every night".

After another lengthy moment of silence where she seemed to be searching for the right words, she finally blurted out, "But, aren't you so bored?"

My eyes widened, and now it was my turn to eat up several seconds with a very awkward silence. All I could think to do was reply with a quick quip, "There's never a dull moment!" and left it at that.

It was one of those moments that I later wished I could've had a do-over. Afterwards, I wished that I had put the question back to her and asked if she had ever been bored as a stay-at-home mother. Not that her question was overtly offensive, but it comes back to my point about the perception that this job is beneath me. Are men somehow overqualified for this work? Why would a man find this whirlwind of activity boring? Babies are a lot of work and it just seemed like a very odd thing to say coming from someone who, not only had kids, but grandkids as well.

That little exchange was actually the exception and not the rule when it came to little old ladies reacting to my status as primary caregiver. Sometimes, I would pack up Abby and head to the mall when it first opened for the day. There, I would stroll her past the shops and stop for a latte or two. The only other people at the mall that early are the old folks who are also there to stroll and sip coffee. They loved to stick their wrinkled apple faces into the stroller to try and elicit a smile from Abby who mostly looked back at them with confused, wide eyes.

"Oh, that's just wonderful! You are truly doing God's work!" is what I once heard from an overly enthusiastic senior citizen. That was certainly high praise, and it was also very indicative of the kind of comments I would routinely get. I would try to take these glowing endorsements in stride and humbly reply that I was just trying to do my part. These remarks were certainly nice to hear, but they were also complete bullshit. Would those little old ladies fawn over a stay-at-home mom who wheeled up beside them and joined them for coffee? I seriously doubted it. One time, after receiving yet another accolade from an elder, I had another one of those "I wish I had a do-over" moments.

If I had the chance to relive the episode, I would have pointed out a slightly frazzled-looking mom in sweat pants who happened to be rolling by our couch at that exact moment with a double-stroller and cried out, "You see that woman and her kids? That's exactly what I do, and she's probably doing a much better job than I am. So stop blowing smoke up my ass!"

OK, I wouldn't have actually said the "stop blowing smoke up my ass" part, as that would have just frightened the gaggle of old people clustered around me, and they were just trying to be nice. But, I think you get the idea. I wasn't doing God's work. I wasn't being heroic. I was just being a regular dad and, speaking of heroic, this brings me to another story that also helps make my point.

On my last day at the office, my colleagues in the marketing department had constructed a life-sized cutout of me … as a superhero. They photoshopped my head onto the body of a man in green spandex and a cape with the words "Super Dad" sprawled across the chest. I thought it was hilarious, as they had found a body that wasn't a typical superhero build. It was rather ordinary, almost flabby, so it actually looked like it could be me squeezed into that ridiculous outfit.

I was carrying my likeness to my car at the end of the day when I ran into a woman who worked upstairs in the purchasing department. She took one look at the foam-core cutout and simply said, "Do the graphic designers also do this for women that go on maternity leave, or do only men get the superhero treatment?" I was pretty sheepish at that moment and mumbled something about having nothing to do with it. In retrospect, I wish that I'd had a longer conversation with her as she was making a good point. Why was I so damn special? Why was I suddenly superhuman for simply staying home to raise my kid? Why was it such a big deal?

I found that most stay-at-home moms I met really didn't make a big deal out of me being a stay-at-home dad and I appreciated that. These women were my comrades, my brothers-in-arms, my fellow soldiers in the battle against diaper rash and dishpan hands. We were all doing the same job, and I respected them and hoped they felt the same way about me. Still, there were a few times when I experienced very different reactions from my fellow domestic engineers. I recall being at the zoo with Abby and a good buddy of mine who also had a very young kid in tow. He was a teacher, and for the summer months he also had the same primary caregiver job. We both knew how to handle small kids, and as we sat down to feed them in the zoo cafeteria we soon found that we were being watched, and perhaps judged.

A couple of lululemon-looking moms approached us about halfway through the meal and gushed, "We just had to come over and say how impressed we are with how you two gentlemen are handling those babies! You wouldn't see our husbands taking kids to the zoo all by themselves. Good for you guys!" We explained our respective situations to the ladies and added that it was actually very common for us to venture out of our homes with little kids, and with no assistance from our better halves. Well, even after hearing that, they still thought that we were such awesome dads, and that we should both be so proud.

I wasn't proud at all. In fact, I think we both rolled our eyes after they turned around and walked back to their table. That little encounter made me wonder if most dads really are that hands-off when it comes to parenting small children. Who can't pack a diaper bag, a couple bottles of milk and survive in the real world for a few hours? I'll admit that if you've never done it before, your first time out without any backup may turn out to be a complete disaster. That's when the typical hands-off dad simply gives up and complains, "You see, honey, I tried to take the kids out without you and it was so hard! Wah, wah, wah!" Gentlemen, I have the solution, and it's simple. Try learning from your mistakes, and every time you go out solo with baby in tow it gets exponentially easier. That's why any man who says he couldn't do what I do is lying through his teeth. He could handle it in a heartbeat. He just doesn't want to do it, as perhaps he feels this "women's work" is beneath him or that he's immensely overqualified for the job. There's a huge difference between can't do it and won't do it.

I have a friend with kids who seems to take great pride in his parenting and domestic ineptitude. His wife works full-time in a professional job, but that doesn't mean they equally share household duties. Whenever she has to leave town for a work conference he makes a strenuous effort via social media to inform the world that taking care of kids just isn't his bag. What do they eat? What's the bedtime routine? How old are they? What are their names? Don't worry, we all get it; you're a man's man who couldn't be bothered to learn basic parenting skills. Yup, we all get it; that stuff is all your wife's domain and any real husband wouldn't be caught dead braiding his daughter's hair. I know that the primary point of his posts were to poke a bit of fun at himself and entertain his audience, but the underlying message of it all is undeniable. It's better to be seen as a clueless dad with his manhood completely intact than some pansy who is fully capable of taking care of his own offspring in his wife's absence.

Now, full disclosure here. I also played that clueless dad card when I first began my new mission at home. I staged several "funny" photographs of me screwing up my first day on the job and emailed them out to all of my friends and family. There was the picture of me changing the wrong end of baby, another one featured me not knowing that SlimFast isn't an appropriate breakfast for baby, and my personal favourite was the shot of me testing the temperature of baby's formula. I had taken some of Lianne's lipstick to create the illusion of massive burn marks on my forearm. This was before the age of Facebook, but it was the same idea. I was implying that I didn't know what I was doing, and I wanted as many people as possible to see it! But in my defense, I only did this particular gag the one time and knew when to give it a rest.

Another example of how other guys view my career choice happened quite recently on the golf course. After being paired up with a couple of guys we didn't know, my buddy and I were asked what we did for a living. My friend chimed in:

"I'm taking the day off of work, but this guy", pointing to me with his seven iron, "he's a stay-at-home dad. Or as I like to call it, semi-retired."

That got a good chuckle from the group, and I simply laughed it off. That certainly wasn't the first time I had heard that gem before, and it likely wouldn't be the last. It did get me thinking though. If a guy stays at home, there is a perception that he must be living on easy street. So much so, the term "semi-retired" is routinely tossed around. Now, think about this. Have you ever heard a stay-at-home mom described that way? I certainly haven't and I wouldn't dream of trying it. As a mini-social experiment, I dare anyone reading this to try it just once. Just blurt this out to the next stay-at-home mom you meet:

"Hey, how does it feel to be semi-retired?"

Then, get back to me and tell me exactly what happened next. I have a feeling it would not end well.

Now that I've taken men to task, let's turn our attention to the fairer sex. I've also encountered women who just assume that a man couldn't possibly understand how hard raising kids can be and mistakenly suspect that I'm also a clueless, hands-off dad who doesn't know what's what! A few years ago, the world went through the H1N1 pandemic scare, and Lianne and I were concerned enough that we decided that our family should get inoculated. The problem was the line-ups to get your shot were exceedingly long, as both the government and the media had whipped everybody into a frenzy. A lot of people were scared that this thing could blow up and be the next Spanish flu, so one chilly winter morning I woke up at 5:30 a.m. to stand in line. The plan was to call and have the family join me when I got close to the front. It was almost noon when I told her to hightail it over to the university and they made it with only a few minutes to spare.

As I was getting the needle stuck into my arm, a rather experienced-looking nurse casually asked how long I had waited in line. I was probably the hundredth person she had asked that morning, and at first, it didn't seem like she was paying much attention to my answer.

'Yup, I bundled up this morning with a whole lotta layers and showed up just before 6:00 a.m. to brave the deep freeze and hold a spot for my family". I added, "I thought I would let them sleep in, and take one for the team."

Her head snapped around to look at me and her terse reaction took me by surprise, "You know, it's no special treat for your wife to stay home and take charge of child care all morning while you simply stand in line."

My response was lighting fast, "Trust me, I know. I've been a stay-at-home dad for years, so I've had more than my fair share!"

The nurse not only didn't say anything in response, but she wouldn't even look at me after our little exchange. She had assumed that she was putting some lazy-ass dad in his place ... someone who obviously never had to watch kids all by his lonesome. I wondered why she would believe that about me, but it all comes back to how society in general views gender roles. How could a man possibly know how hard raising kids can be? How indeed.

I did find that there was one particular segment of society that had the most trouble relating to my line of work, and that was the old men. I love to golf, and on rare occasions I would drop off Abby at my parents' house and try and play nine holes as a "single." Since all of my regular playing partners worked during the day, I would just show up at the golf course and hope to join up with an existing twosome or threesome. One day, I was sent off with these three old guys, and I mean old guys. I bet none of them were a day under ninety, but they were still very active and two of them didn't even use a golf cart. A couple of them would actually tee up the ball from the fairway, but who was I to call them out on this major rule infraction?

After playing the first few holes in relative silence, one of them turned to me after a pretty decent approach shot and asked, "So, what do you do for a living, young man?"

I quickly and loudly replied, "I've been a stay-at-home dad for a few years now."

He paused for a moment and then asked again, "But what do you do?"

Thinking he wanted to know the specifics of my daily routine, I answered, "Well, it's not all that exciting, but I've got kid-duty, do the laundry, shop for groceries. You know, all of the household stuff."

He started to look a bit flustered now. He squinted his eyes underneath his weathered Jack Nicklaus "Golden Bear" visor, squeezed my forearm with his tanned, age-spotted hand and firmly asked again, "No, I want to know what you do for a living!"

I finally figured it out! He wanted to know what I did prior to being at home.

"Oh, sorry about that", I chucked, "I spent about 5 years working in broadcast journalism, and then five more in advertising…"

But he wouldn't even let me finish my sentence. As soon as he heard journalism, his ears perked up. "My son has worked almost twenty years as a newspaper man. He's now city editor and loves every minute of it."

After that, the conversation was very fluid. Once he had a way to relate to me, he was quite the chatty Cathy, and he seemed very interested to hear about my experiences writing for TV news. But for whatever reason he had no way to connect with me if I was just a stay-at-home dad.

I also found my parents guilty of giving people of the "older generation" my full résumé and employment history when they spoke of me. They'd tell their friends that I was indeed a stay-at-home dad, but there was always plenty of follow-up information to be relayed. "Greg actually has two university degrees, one in English and the other in Journalism," they would assert. "He worked in broadcasting and advertising, and has only been at home for a few years... yadda, yadda, yadda."

You might think that I'd be mildly offended by the notion that being a stay-at-home dad isn't impressive in its own right. Why did my folks have to throw in all of that other stuff about my past accomplishments? Is what I do for a living not good enough? Maybe I should feel snubbed by it, but, to be honest with you, I'm not. The truth is, I have been just as guilty of playing up my previous work experience when I talk about my current employment situation.

I'M DOING ALL RIGHT

I normally wouldn't give a complete stranger the bullet points of my résumé when introducing myself, but I did find myself doing just that in the early days of my life at home. It wasn't a regular occurrence, but rather it was reserved for those times when I was at one of Lianne's work functions, law firm retreats or other events where highly paid professionals would congregate. Somehow, it made a difference when I was surrounded by people who employed live-in nannies as, technically, I was our family's live-in nanny. I've was actually approached by one of Lianne's work friends about taking on their kids – perhaps even starting a day home. I was mortified and incredulous at the mere thought of adding other people's kids to my plate. Was this really how people now saw me? Being thought of as simply a child-care professional was a little hard on the ego at first. But, I discontinued the silly practice of making sure everyone met knew I was once a "real" professional fairly early on, as I was becoming more comfortable with my new gig with every passing day. I also stopped because I had a new side project that was quite "manly," thus countering my domestic duties and giving me something else to play up after letting someone know I was a stay-at-home dad.

As Abby grew bigger and more mobile, she was amassing a rather large amount of baby toys and accessories. Our home started to resemble a toy store. At first, we had piled up a bunch of baby stuff in a small area behind our couch, but that soon became overloaded. Our next solution was to move the dining room table into our unfinished basement, and create a play area. There was only one problem - the hanging light fixture that was normally placed directly above the centre of the table. It now hung about four and a half feet above the floor. Guess what happens when you are sitting down with your baby for twenty minutes and suddenly jump up to get the phone? CLANG! "AHHHHHHRGGG, my head!"

I don't know how I never completely smashed the glass in the fixture or my skull, as I must have hit that stupid light ten times. To make matters worse, the entire main floor of our house was starting to look like a perpetual chaotic play zone. We were a growing family and needed more space, so we decided to enlist my uber-handy father to finish the basement. Swinging hammers, framing walls, hanging drywall, installing doors and cutting baseboards was all very masculine and it gave my ego a temporary testosterone boost.

For about six months, my dad and I worked away in the basement while my mom looked after little Abby. We did a lot of the work ourselves, but I did subcontract the plumbing, electrical and painting. Dad was all about the planning, the measuring and the cutting. Once the studs or sheets of drywall were tacked in, I would step in with my hammer or power screwdriver and finish up. I'm not all that handy, but I take orders very well. I'm a married man, remember? (Sorry folks, not all the jokes are winners.) After the paint dried and we moved everything in, our newly finished basement looked great. Lianne and I reclaimed our main floor, restoring it to its pre-baby motif. The renovation was complete, but I no longer needed it as some kind of crutch to balance my role as primary caregiver. I also didn't feel the need to explain to people how I used to have a "regular" career before this.

It was starting to sink in that it wasn't only the child-rearing element that was important; it was completing the daily household chores that really made me an asset.

Lianne works in corporate securities law, a profession that can get insanely busy and very stressful. While I've never professed to be a truly effective homemaker, Lianne appreciated that she didn't have to start dinner or fold clothes when she came home from a particularly tough day at the office. Helping keep our home life on track really does make a difference, and it ends up being an essential service. What made me feel even more crucial to the success of our operation was a story about another stay-at-home dad relayed to me by a friend.

Let's call this guy "Paul" to protect his identity. Paul's life and mine are only similar if you barely scratch the surface, but, if you dig deeper, you find our lives could not be more polar opposite. Like me, he's a stay-at-home father while his wife toils away in the banking profession. Unlike me, Paul doesn't seem to have any actual responsibilities and spends his days having coffee with friends, training for triathlons and taking sculpting classes. When they had another baby, they hired a nanny... a NANNY! What exactly is his purpose in that family? Not only did they have a nanny when the kids were young, Paul's wife still had to cook meals when she came home from work, do the laundry and run the house.

Hearing about this guy actually made me feel manlier than ever. I was stepping up! I was making a contribution! I was making spaghetti and meatballs! I could not imagine adding to my wife's burden of being the sole family breadwinner by forcing her to handle household chores when she wasn't busy paying for the roof above our head and the shoes on our feet. I asked my friend how this "Paul" could possibly get away with this. He surmised that perhaps his wife thinks he's a real catch and is lucky to have him. Wow was all I could say to that. I sometimes feel guilty that I'm not doing enough around the house, but compared to that guy I discovered that I'm doing all right.

WUMP, WUMP, WUMP, WUMP

I want to stress again that I am no superstar when it comes to running a tight ship, but I am slowly but surely improving. Laundry is the bane of my existence, and I struggle to keep ahead of a usually overflowing clothes hamper. In our first house, we had the old-fashioned top-loading washer and dryer. If you lift the lid, you see in bold letters: DO NOT OVERLOAD. Bah! That's for wussies who are scared of their own shadow. I'll put as many pairs of jeans in there as I want, thank you very much.

Fast-forward to a particularly heavy load that almost made the washer drum eject from its white metal housing. Lianne and I were on the main floor, and all you could hear was a bone-rattling WUMP, WUMP, WUMP, WUMP coming from the top floor! It was the final spin cycle, and the washing machine was violently lurching to the side, banging the adjacent dryer over and over again. I debated turning off the machine, but I saw by the dial that the cycle was almost complete. So, I waited through three more minutes of a house-shaking WUMP, WUMP, WUMP, WUMP and then very nonchalantly moved the clothes into the dryer and came down the stairs. Lianne gave me a very unimpressed look, and I totally deserved it. That was the last time I overloaded that particular washing machine to that extreme, but I always made sure the load was slightly over capacity. Old habits die hard, and that's why I was very pleased when we purchased a front-loading stackable washer and dryer set in our next home. I almost squealed with delight when I was reading the instruction manual and found out the truly impressive load capacity of this wonderful new machine. It boasted that it could handle fourteen pairs of jeans in one wash. Fourteen pairs? Damn! My massive laundry load days were back, baby!

Everything was working according to plan, as there seemed no limit to the amount of clothes I could wash in a single load, except that one time. Have you ever put a large load into the washing machine, then promptly forgot about it for two or three days? Probably not, but this is me we're talking about. When I realized my mistake, I simply thought that I should run this heavy, dank, soaked-in load that was very likely at the upper limit of the machine's load capacity AGAIN. Lianne and I were in the basement watching TV, and there was that violent sound again: WUMP, WUMP, WUMP, WUMP! I obviously had experience with this wumping, so I paused the TV, ran upstairs to the laundry room and was absolutely stunned at what I saw.

That massive, wet load in the spin cycle had moved the stacked washer and dryer about four feet from the wall, ripping off the dryer vent hose in the process! I quickly shut the washer off, and was shocked that the vibrations could have moved two heavy appliances that far. The fact that I had such a hard time pushing them back into place was a testament to the sheer power and force of that spin cycle, and my idiotic plan of putting a huge load of already wet clothes into a washing machine and simply hoping for the best. I reconnected the dryer vent and put the load in the dryer and went back downstairs, pretending like nothing out of the ordinary happened.

When I plopped back down on the sectional couch, Lianne looked at me with a slight frown and asked, "What took you so long?"

"Ah, I was just moving the wet clothes into the dryer... and you know, maybe I overloaded the washer just a little bit? So yeah, that's why we heard that slight wumping sound. No biggie. It's all good."

"If you say so", she replied, still looking at me with just a hint of disbelief in her eyes.

I was praying that she didn't notice the glistening beads of sweat on my forehead which were a direct result of my struggle to slide a very heavy washer and dryer back into place. I was embarrassed, but, a couple of years later, I finally gave my wife all of the gory details of this incident and received yet another well-deserved unimpressed look.

While I have learned from my laundry blunders, that doesn't mean I've mastered the fine art of keeping ahead of the soiled apparel game. On more than one occasion I've received a gentle reminder from Lianne that she's down to two pairs of clean underwear, or my daughter will scold me when she is completely out of panties. Even when I do the laundry, it's possible a huge pile of clean socks and undies will sit in a laundry basket, unfolded, for several days. When I get the angry yell, "Daddy, you didn't do the laundry!" I will defiantly yell back that I most certainly did, but you'll have to root through the basket to find a matching pair of socks! That will teach anyone to doubt me.

I remember when a basket of clean clothes sat on the laundry room floor for such an extended period of time that we almost completely emptied its contents, thus solving the whole "folding" issue. So, yes, there have been times when I have fallen off the wagon and have been remiss in my duties. It's only happened a few times in all of the years that I've been staying home, but I know that I've totally screwed up when I hear the washing machine start up without me. I will run to the laundry room to find Lianne washing clothes! I'll protest that I don't want her doing the laundry because that's MY job. "Then do it," she'll quip. Touché.

I actually have an annoying catch phrase for when I find my wife doing something I have deemed my responsibility. I'll say, "Are you trying to be a hero?" if she starts to unpack the dishwasher. Then I'll shoo her away and do it myself. If I forget to buy milk, I will actually wait for her to get home from work, and then I'll dash to the convenience store to get a fresh jug. She'll ask why I didn't ask her to stop on the way home and pick some up and my response is always the same. "That's not your job." It's not that hard to keep milk in the fridge, fold clothes or load and unload the dishwasher. These are all things I should be doing during the day with the greatest of ease. Before starting a family, Lianne and I divided all household chores because we were both working, but these days I want to truly earn my keep. I would like my hardworking wife to have a bit of downtime when she isn't working like a dog. I don't consider her time unloading the dishwasher as "downtime".

Over the years, people have asked Lianne if I really do all of the housework, cooking and cleaning and she always says yes. But, there's always a small pause before she answers. Yes, I'm doing all of that, but no I'm not winning any awards for making the most delicious or healthy meals, keeping the house in tip-top shape or staying ahead of the laundry. Sometimes our refrigerator looks like a barren wasteland, or Abby is wearing a pair of pants that is obviously two sizes too small. I know she must have thought this more than once, but thankfully, Lianne has never actually asked me,

"Just what have you been DOING all day???"

She's confided to friends that there have been times when we have run out of milk for the second time in a week and she has to bite her tongue. She doesn't want to be a nag, or appear to be giving me pointers on how to run a household, but I'm sure she would agree that my occasional ineptitude can be frustrating. I think her biggest challenge has been to lower her standards and just let me do things my way. In those first few years of me running the household, it was especially difficult for her not to nitpick or second-guess my decisions. Lianne would have never said these things out loud, but I'm sure she thought them:

"That's not the way would have folded that shirt."

"That's not what I would have made for school lunch."

"That's not the outfit I would have chosen Abby to wear to that birthday party."

All of that being said, Lianne knows there's a method to my madness, and will always wrap up any evaluation of my work performance with, "At least Greg's doing the job, and that means that I don't have to."

It isn't exactly high praise, but I'll take it.

THE DOUBLE STANDARD

Early on in my domestic role, I recall getting a knock at the door on a day when our main floor looked like a tornado had just ripped through it. These were the days before our finished basement and there were toys everywhere. To make matters worse, the sink was overflowing with dirty dishes and there were sections of the newspaper strewn all over the floor. We had an "open concept" main floor, so almost all of this was visible from the front door. My visitor turned out to be the wife of one of my best friends, and I can't remember what she was dropping off. I just remember being very embarrassed by the state of my home and holding the door open just enough to carry on a short conversation while desperately trying to block her view of the mess behind me. If she moved her head to try and catch a glimpse, I would mirror her movements and keep my body placed squarely in front of hers. Eventually, she left and I knew I had been busted. I was a total and complete slob.

I'm convinced that if you compare the job that I'm doing with ninety-nine stay-at-home moms, I would very likely rank close to the bottom of the pack. If a woman had my culinary skills, my penchant for allowing us to run out of clean underwear and my ability to let a mess stew for days, she would be considered a terrible stay-at-home parent. Yet, somehow, if a man does all of that he gets a ticker-tape parade. It's an incredible double standard that gives us guys a free pass to be less than stellar in our daily household duties. I get all of the credit in the world just for trying, and that can actually work against me. In my case, it means that the bar has been set pretty low, as Lianne is happy that we have a parent who stays home, is there after school and goes to music, gymnastics and soccer practices. After that, she's learned not to expect me to be Martha Stewart.

The fact that my best meals are the ones that I purchase from a place down the street that makes daily gourmet meals is irrelevant. I have it easier because I don't think I face the same expectations that a stay-at-home mom would have. The stress of homemaking is something that I've never really experienced because I believe the job is as hard as you want to make it. If it's paramount that your home be spotless, every home-cooked meal be planned out days ahead of time and you have to look great while doing it, then I can see how this job could completely stress you out. That would be a lot of pressure. While I don't speak for all househusbands, I can't shake the feeling that most guys in my position simply don't feel the same pressure as our female counterparts.

An interesting study published in 2000 in the academic journal *Contemporary Family Therapy* reports that stay-at-home moms are both more stressed and exhausted than stay-at-home dads. It suggests that women are socialized in our society to put the needs of others ahead of their own. Mothers may spend much of their time tending to the needs of their kids and hubby at the expense of their own. On the flipside, stay-at-home dads may feel less guilt about taking care of themselves and therefore be better able to justify time for "relaxation and self-renewal." Amen to that, brother. I know that makes me sound a tad selfish, but I really have no problem putting off washing a load of dirty kids clothing so I can take an extended coffee break.

I also don't really care about keeping up appearances. Lianne is a total clothes horse. She has the giant walk-in closet to prove it, and the sleek, svelte figure to justify it. She always looks very stylish, whether she's in her sharp business attire or cool casual wardrobe. For a forty-something year-old-man, the way I dress for my job is borderline embarrassing, with ball caps, worn-out tee shirts, and ripped jeans accentuating my personal style. I have actually driven to school drop-off wearing pajama bottoms. I know that not all stay-at-home moms have the time to doll themselves up every day, but I'm sure the vast majority of them don't wear the same pair of pants three days in a row. I don't think anyone is keeping track of what I wear each day, but even if they did, it wouldn't bother me one bit. Actually, there's not a whole lot that bothers me.

When I was still working in advertising, I would sometimes have trouble getting to sleep at night. My head was spinning with deadlines and work stress, and I would toss and turn for a couple of hours before I could finally nod off. Since I've been home, I sleep like a baby. Sure, I sometimes worry about house stuff, the future or if I'm doing a good parenting job, but the home stress is somehow different. It doesn't keep me awake at night.

I could be wrong, but I also think that stay-at-home parents who didn't previously work outside of the home may have a very different take on how to run a household. I feel if being a stay-at-home parent is the only job you've ever had, you may tackle the challenges of the day much more earnestly.

My office life was so structured and deadline oriented, but my home life could not be more different. There's not a whole lot of planning that goes into my day. I sometimes run out of time to get all of my errands done, and I suddenly realize that I didn't plan anything for dinner. Is this a disaster? Not for me. Who wants pizza?! Most days, I'm just making it up as I go along. But, if you compare how I handled my job in the early years to my current situation, you will find that I've come a long way after more than a decade on duty. The bottom line is, just being a guy makes this job a whole lot easier in many respects, but not all of them. Being born with the XY chromosome will cut you a lot of slack, but sometimes being a stay-at-home parent in a profession dominated by women can kind of suck.

I'D CHECK OUT WHEN THE TOPIC BECAME "LACTATION RELATED"

There aren't many people like me out there, and that's something I've learned very quickly after starting my life at home. I mentioned before that Lianne was part of a "mommy group" when she was home with Abby for the first six months. Did I inherit her spot in this little club? No, I did not, but I'm not so sure I ever wanted it. It's not easy to be the only guy in a large group of ladies, but that's the situation that I have found myself in time after time.

Most stay-at-home moms have a built-in social network of other moms that can be called upon for childcare, play dates, coffee dates, or simply for empathy. Most stay-at-home dads don't get that experience, and I think that leads to isolation. That's not to say that all moms are doing their best to exclude me because I've made some pretty good friends over the years. It's actually more my issue, as I've never felt all that comfortable navigating through that world. It seemed other moms would hang out and chat after our "Music with Baby" classes, exchanging stories and phone numbers, while I would quickly pack up my little Ab-flab and get the hell out of Dodge.

My brother and his family have lived overseas for quite a while and were part of the "ex-pat community" wherever they lived. Usually, that meant the husband worked, while the wife hung out with other similar wives. My sister-in-law told me a story about one couple who broke the ex-pat mold. The wife was the breadwinner, so the husband was the one hanging out with a group of women. He was eventually accepted as one of the gang and found the entire experience to be fascinating, garnering him incredible insight into the lives of the fairer sex. His group of girlfriends would eventually divulge their secrets, and he ultimately became somewhat of an expert on inter-marital relationships. He was one of the few husbands out there who had an *in*, and actually knew what a woman meant when she said that "nothing was wrong." As interesting as that may seem, I never strived for that experience.

I remember hanging with a group of moms at the playground after pre-school was let out. I knew all of them well enough, and was actually fairly comfortable chit-chatting, but now and then the conversation would turn to a subject matter not appropriate for all audiences. I would check out when the topic became "lactation related." It was at times like that I would wonder what it would be like to have a gaggle of guy friends, all full-time parents.

One of my best friends is leading a parallel life to mine, but 2,000 kilometres away in the great state of Minnesota. I've known James my entire life and, like me, he is a stay-at-home dad. Instead of marrying a lawyer, he married a doctor and has two kids and shares many of my experiences and struggles. He once told me about a group of men that his wife had found out about. They were all stay-at-home dads who met in a park once a week for a giant play date. They were also complete strangers, but, at the urging of his wife, he agreed to meet up with them. I asked him how the "Dads Date" went and if he was going to go back the next week. His answer was short and sweet, "Nah, they all seemed like a bunch of nerds."

It would be great if my old pal James lived in my hometown, as it would be nice to have someone to shoot the shit with and swap stories. We do chat a fair bit on the phone, and we've been on several joint get-togethers involving both families, but it would be that much better to have another guy who has walked a mile in my shoes right here in Calgary.

I've actually met a few other stay-at-home dads over the years, either at school or other extra-curricular activities, but I never felt any connection or urge to make any of them a new buddy. I think most guys know pretty damn quickly if they want to hang with someone or not. This raises an interesting question about the differences between how men and women who stay at home interact with other parents. Are women more likely to "suffer fools" for the sake of ensuring their kids have an active social life? Maybe. I've chatted with a couple of stay-at-home moms who have described painfully awkward afternoons with women they barely knew, all so little Suzie can play barbies with little Sara. I think there's more of an expectation that women should always accept those play date invitations, or risk being forever labeled as rude, snobby or not family-friendly. I don't think men face nearly the same scrutiny, and to be honest, that was huge relief. It's not that I was anti-social or unable to handle interactions with new people ... I was just lazy and sometimes couldn't be bothered with the time and effort that comes with scheduling friendship-time for my daughter.

My lack of integration into the preschool mommy circles also meant that my kid didn't get nearly the amount of play dates as other kids, and this would lead to me getting an earful from an angry four-year-old girl. When your child is barely out of toddlerhood, play dates are not of the "drop off and take off" variety. You actually have to stay and chat over coffee while the kids play. Being a dude meant the invites were few and far between. Most of the blame was squarely on my shoulders, as I was making zero effort to put myself out there and squeeze my way into a new social clique.

It turns out, while sometimes I feel alone, I'm not alone in feeling … alone. Remember the study I referenced earlier that was published in *Contemporary Family Therapy*? It also suggests that stay-at-home dads are less likely to network or volunteer in their community and were less involved with activities outside the home. Fewer fathers socialized with other stay-at-home parents and would often describe themselves as an outsider. The study also showed that stay-at-home dads are also less likely to find other men who stay at home to share experiences and may prefer isolation to socializing with stay-at-home moms. Because the stay-at-home dad is still a fairly new phenomenon in our society, the study says they find fewer opportunities to network with people with they can identify with. All of this begs the question – why are so many of us stay-at-home dads wandering all alone, out in the wilderness when we could be building a village with other moms? The study suggests its findings could be attributed in part to the way men are socialized to be independent and able to handle things on their own. If you ask me, I think a lot of men are just too damn lazy to make the effort. Or maybe that's just me?

This feeling of me being a man apart was magnified even more because it seemed everything school-related was also very gender-specific, and very encouraging of defined roles for mothers and fathers. We attend a private Catholic school, and it's obvious that a traditional family structure is the model. I would get emails from the school asking me to attend a monthly "Men's Leadership Breakfast." It was designed for the business leaders to meet downtown and exchange ideas. Lianne was actually qualified to attend that kind of meeting, but instead she would receive invites to an afternoon "Ladies Spa for the Soul."

Lianne was invited to join the school parents' social committee, and she accepted, but explained that she may not be able to attend all of the meetings and volunteered me to be her alternate. Well, Lianne may have attended one or two meetings off the start, but then it soon became apparent that I was now a full-time member of this committee. It was comprised of ten lovely ladies and yours truly. I actually went to the monthly meetings for a year and then quietly pulled the pin. I really had no interest in helping to plan "Pasta Night," but I did enjoy the free coffee and doughnuts. Instead of sitting on the committee, I decided that I could better serve our school by volunteering to drive and help supervise any and all field trips.

So, it may not seem like a huge downside, but literally feeling like the odd man out can be the most challenging part of my job. The good news is that as time goes on, it has definitely become less of an issue. Either I'm feeling more accepted, or perhaps I'm just putting myself out there more often.

MILLION DOLLAR FAMILY

By now, you've noticed that this account of my decade-long tenure as a stay-at-home dad isn't quite chronological in its telling. I've occasionally jumped forward and back in time as I describe some of the experiences I've had along the way. You may have also noticed from time to time, I've been using purposefully vague language when describing the make-up of our family. I'd like to set the record straight right here, right now. We have two kids, and this next chapter describes our journey to double our baby output.

Abby was now over a year old and was certainly a handful. Once she took those first few steps as an upright human being, she was off and running and it was my job to simply try and keep up. As our baby girl was rapidly morphing into a little girl, we never once thought that she would be our only foray into child rearing. The plan was always to have two kids, maybe even three. Having both grown up with siblings, Lianne and I thought that giving Abby the same experience was the way to go. We felt the need to get cracking sooner rather than later because of that darned biological clock. By now, Lianne was almost thirty-five, and she sensed the ticking was getting louder with each passing day.

Now that we were seasoned professionals at conceiving, Lianne dug up her charting materials and we once again started tracking her ovulation cycle. The lengthy (but ultimately rewarding) formula of putting bun #1 in the oven was still very fresh in my mind. While the drawn-out program may have frustrated Lianne at times, it completely invigorated a slightly neglected aspect of our marriage that I thought needed a little jump start. I presumed that putting bun #2 into the oven might not take nine months, or even six months, but I was cautiously optimistic that I had just punched my golden ticket to several months of regularly scheduled "programming."

I can still remember that mid-summer night in 2004 when Lianne had finished up her first monthly chart and determined that she was very likely too late in her cycle to try and conceive. I strenuously intervened with a very unscientific argument to try and change her mind, "But, hey, you never know!" That was the best case I could make, but it didn't matter because it worked. Now when I say "it worked"… I mean my plea for sex was granted, but I also mean we hit the jackpot with just one pull of the slot machine. I'm not kidding around.

Child number one was conceived after nine months of trying, while child number two took all of nine minutes, maybe less! When we confirmed our suspicions about a week later with a home pregnancy test, a small part of me was proud of my amazing accuracy proclaiming, "My boys knew right where to go!" A much larger part of me knew that golden ticket I thought I had punched had just been revoked, but no matter. We were both over the moon about being officially pregnant with baby number two and excited for another chapter of our family life to begin.

As the days and weeks of the new pregnancy went by, both Lianne and I began to dread the unappealing reality that we'd have to endure all of those sleepless nights, late night feedings and bouts of extreme exhaustion all over again. Correction: Lianne would have to endure all of those sleepless nights, late night feedings and bouts of extreme exhaustion, but I would obviously do what I could to make those crazy first few months a little bit easier for her. When Abby was born, I was still a working stiff, and I only took two weeks of vacation time to help out. This time, I would be home full-time, and together we would both be omnipresent to tackle the challenges of raising a toddler and a newborn head-on, at least for Lianne's six-month maternity leave.

Speaking of the "first few months," it would appear that my wife was going through a carbon copy of her first pregnancy. There was the same morning sickness, the same aches and pains and, of course, the uncomfortable sleeps. She even carried baby number two the same way - all up front. By the end of nine months, we were more than ready for our new addition to make a grand entrance. Once again, we didn't find out what we were having, ensuring our gender-neutral yellow-hued nursery was ready to go, no matter what popped out.

When Abby arrived on the scene, Lianne kept working at her day job almost right up to the delivery, and this time was no different. While baby number one ended up being a few days late, baby number two wanted to break out a few days early. The date was March 1, 2005, and it started out just like the day before, but by around midday Lianne started having contractions. Now, being the old pros at childbirth that we were, nobody was hitting the panic button just yet. The thirty-hour ordeal that was Abby's arrival was only two years in the past, but it felt like it was just yesterday. We knew that this could be a very lengthy process, and we were ready for the long haul.

Unlike the first time we made a special delivery, I wasn't religiously timing the contractions, but I did notice that they were coming fairly consistently and about five to seven minutes apart. I remember laughing at Lianne as she took one final work phone call that afternoon. Every few minutes, she would put her hand over the "speaking end" of the handset and make a very pained expression, all while keeping her ear pressed against the other end so she could still listen to the conversation. Watching someone try to carry on a serious legal discussion while having regular contractions was very entertaining, but it was around that time when I noticed they were coming even faster than before. I casually mentioned that maybe we should go to the hospital to get her checked out. Lianne's response was swift and crystal clear, "I don't want to drive all the way there just to be sent home like last time! Trust me, I know my body and I know it is not time to go."

I'd learned over our near nine years of marriage that it was futile to engage in a serious debate with my wife when she took a firm stance on an issue. Tack on the fact that she was nine months pregnant and having painfully annoying contractions, I decided to drop the issue for the time being. I wasn't going to change her mind right then and there, but in less than an hour it became a moot point.

We had made arrangements for my parents to come over and take little Abby back to their place for a sleepover as we didn't need an active toddler tripping us up as we made our way to the maternity ward. Lianne was starting to really feel those ever-increasing earthquakes emanating from her loins, so I decided to call my parents to come over as soon as they could. I remember my dad answering the phone and explaining that Mom was at a hair appointment, and he wanted to wait for her to come home so they could arrive together. I made it obvious that he had to drop whatever he was doing, leave Mom behind and hightail it over to our place as soon as humanly possible!

I couldn't believe that I became the voice of reason or that Lianne actually listened to me when I boldly proclaimed, "The second my dad arrives, we are so out of here!" At this point, Lianne was in no condition to disagree, and we were out the door and on the road the moment Abby was picked up and whisked away. Thankfully, the hospital was about a five-minute drive from our house. But, that didn't stop a much panicked thought from crossing my mind: "Are we going to make it to the hospital before this baby comes out?" Yes, the contractions were coming that fast and furious!

We made our way to the maternity ward as quickly as we could, and in no time Lianne was zipped into an examination room and lying flat on her back. After a quick look-see from the nurse, we all knew the verdict; she was fully dilated and was ready to be moved into a delivery room. The only problem was they didn't have an open delivery room for us, so Lianne and I were forced to wait it out in the examination room while the frequency and intensity of the contractions kept escalating. Everything was happening so fast that when the nurse suggested that I make my way to the administration desk to check Lianne into the hospital, I simply obliged. On my way there, I couldn't shake the feeling that I shouldn't have left Lianne's side. After discovering that the main administration office closes at 5:00 p.m., I was redirected to the E.R. administration desk, which was a bit of a hike from the maternity ward. As I impatiently waited in line, I hoped I wouldn't miss our baby's grand entrance. I finally made it to the front of the line and had a seat across from a hospital admitting staff member, separated by a glass partition. Shortly after I sat down, the woman taking my information stood up and said she needed to grab another form for me to fill out. Just seconds after she left, the woman in the next cubicle answered a phone, looked to her left, and then looked to her right. After making eye contact with me, she yelled through the glass, "Is your name Greg?" I nodded, and she said, "You've got to go, NOW!"

As I sprinted down the long hospital hallways, I had a sudden pang of regret … I knew I shouldn't have left her alone! What if I miss it? As I repeatedly tapped the "up" button in the elevator lobby I kept wondering just what the hell was happening with my wife. As it turned out, quite a lot!

I later learned that just minutes after I left Lianne behind to check her in to the hospital, a couple of nurses began moving her to a delivery room by helping her slowly shuffle down the hallway. I guess Lianne was stopping during the nearly constant contractions and really feeling the urge to push. The nurses kept warning her that if she didn't get a move on, she might have the baby in the hallway!

As soon as Lianne arrived in the delivery room, she was ready to pop. Just before they started, Lianne interrupted the proceedings by demanding an epidural, but a nurse quickly dismissed the urgent request stating, "We don't have time!" Lianne definitely didn't like that answer and blurted out, "You don't understand; I can't have this baby without drugs!" The nursed countered, "YOU don't understand; this baby is coming right now! It's time to push!"

Almost completely out of breath, I stumbled into the maternity ward from the E.R. I then quickly realized that I had no idea where Lianne was. When I left her, she was still in an examination room. Intuitively, they must have been expecting a sweaty-looking man with a crazed look in his eye to arrive on the scene because there was a nurse directing me to the delivery room with one of those "windmill" arm motions that a traffic cop would use, pointing me in the right direction. As I burst into the room, I pulled back the curtain and my jaw dropped. There was Lianne, and there was the baby, already head and shoulders out of the birth canal! As I made my way into the room, my lovely wife made one final push and our son Daniel was born. I had barely been in the room for half a minute before the doctor handed me the snippers and asked if I wanted to cut the cord. As I sliced through that rubbery cable, a huge sense of relief washed over me ... I made it. Yes, it was insanely close, but I definitely made it back in time to witness the birth of our second child.

As the delivery team was cleaning and wrapping up our brand-new, pink, wrinkly son, one of the nurses asked if we had any other kids. I said we had a two-year-old girl as well, and she replied, "Oh that's wonderful; now you have a million dollar family!" I just smiled back, but was too embarrassed to ask what she meant. I had heard the term before, but wasn't quite sure how it applied to our family. When we got home the next day, I used the google machine to look it up. Million dollar family: one girl, one boy. We had one of each flavor and our family of four was now complete.

MEET THE NEW BOSS, SAME AS THE OLD BOSS

Both Lianne and I were really looking forward to six months of bonding as a new family of four. Unlike last time, I would be there right from the start, sharing the load, the love and the laughter of what was sure to be a wonderful experience and a much-needed break for Lianne from her high-stress job. With Abby, Lianne had to deal with very long, lonely days stuck at home with a screaming baby, but this time was supposed to be different. This time was supposed to be awesome. What we got was a new boss, same as the old boss.

It would appear that my wife's body is capable of producing just one very specific size of baby. When our newborn Daniel Clarke was weighed and measured, we were more than a little surprised when they wrote down 7 pounds, 11 ounces, and 22 centimetres long. Hey! Those were the exact same stats of our firstborn! The only tiny difference between our two babies' measurements was a half-centimetre disparity in head circumference.

That was certainly a happy coincidence and a neat little conversation starter. But, after the first few weeks of life at home with our new son unfolded, it was apparent that Daniel also shared another trait with his older sister; however, this one was anything but neat. Once again, the parenting gods decided to test our mettle by bestowing us the great honour of having another colicky baby. Wait. WHAT? How could this happen to us all over again? Who did we piss off to deserve another loud, stressful and supremely annoying half year of our lives? During the pregnancy, we joked about having to endure another colicky baby, but we would quickly laugh and brush off the suggestion as ludicrous. What were the odds? I guess they were way better than we could have ever imagined. I actually consulted the google machine on this very topic, and there does not appear to be any link between first-born colicky babies and second born babies having a higher percentage chance of developing colic. I guess we were just lucky to hit the colic jackpot twice in a row.

The magical moments we had hoped for were few and far between, but Lianne was determined to try and right the ship. During the first go around, we tried some of the suggested solutions to ease colic symptoms, but to no avail. This time, Lianne redoubled her research efforts and was hoping that a dietary change would make a difference. It was theorized that a mother's diet could affect her breast milk and be one of the determining factors in why some babies are prone to colic. I felt terrible for her as she ate boiled chicken and bland rice every day for a month, hoping against hope that it would make a difference. It didn't.

The reaction of our two-year-old daughter to having a brand new baby brother only made matters worse. Before Daniel arrived on the scene, our firstborn had morphed into a wonderful little toddler! Abby started to talk at an early age, so she was very verbal and quite happy-go-lucky. For the most part, she was a fun bundle of energy that was actually pretty easy to manage. That didn't last long once we brought home her pink and wrinkly brother wrapped up in a blanket. The first sign of trouble came the moment we tried to get a picture of the two of them together. Abby wanted no part of that tiny sibling. Can we put Daniel on your lap? Can you give your baby brother a kiss on the head? Can you sit beside him on the couch while Mommy holds him? "NO! NO! and NO!" were the answers to any suggestion we had that day.

It wasn't like Abby was cruel to the newest member of our family. Rather, she simply refused to acknowledge his existence. It's like he was Israel and she was Palestine: Daniel did not have the right to settle in the sacred land that was our happy home. The shake-up in our home's make-up also brought out a new personality trait in Abby that rarely surfaced - whining. She whined about everything and seemed to complain about anything. I guess they call it the terrible twos for a reason, but we wanted our little sweetheart back!

Looking back, it was really no surprise that a firstborn child would have her nose bent out of shape over the arrival of a newborn. That happens a lot when a family grows, but in our case we really could have used a sweet, doting "big sister" who wanted to smother her new brother with love. That might have made things run a tad smoother in our household.

A big part of the problem was Abby's lack of sleep during the day. We always boasted about our kids' ability to sleep through the night at an early age and take very scheduled naps. But at two years old, Abby decided that she no longer needed to nap. I knew of kids who were six that still wanted to nap every afternoon, but not our daughter. Nope. She figured her two stressed out parents who were coping with a colicky newborn would truly appreciate their older child's decision to stop napping and launch a new whining/complaining campaign. So, this is what we ended up with as the weeks dragged into months.

As I stated earlier, it's not like our lives were 100 per cent awful, as even colicky babies have some good days now and then. Looking back at the photos and videos of that time, one would have never known that we were smack dab in the middle of the lowest and most challenging point in our marriage. When Abby arrived, I went to my corporate job during her first six months of life, and I didn't experience the lion's share of the stress of being with an infant who was fussy a majority of her waking hours. This time, I felt the full brunt of it all. It was a trifecta that left us all in a fairly unhappy place: a crying baby, a super-whiny toddler and a stressed-out wife who just wanted her last chance at an extended leave from work to be somewhat enjoyable.

After the dust settled on Daniel's first half year of life, things ended up working themselves out. The colic slowly diminished at the four-month mark, and once Daniel grew out of his "helpless lump" phase and started sitting up and moving around on his own, we saw a huge change in his big sister's attitude. Suddenly, her baby brother was very interesting and worth a second look. They became best buddies and remain very close to this day.

Both Lianne and I survived parenting two colicky kids and hoped the pain and suffering we went through at this early stage would somehow be balanced out by a cakewalk in the troublesome teenage years. During our endless research on colic, we also learned that it's theorized by some that babies with colic have higher IQs as adults. We were simply hoping there was some kind of payoff for the extra stress we had to put up with, something that will make it all worthwhile. It turned out that there was a fringe benefit after all.

PARENTING STRATEGIES: HITS AND MISSES

The fact that both of our babies were excellent sleepers and nappers during their long months of their colic literally saved our sanity. Right from the get-go, both Abby and Daniel were sleeping in their crib and not squished between us in our matrimonial bed. The first couple of months of constant nighttime feedings were obviously rough on Lianne, but once those kids started sleeping through the night and were getting regularly scheduled naps during the day, our lives got a whole lot easier.

However, that happy circumstance didn't just happen by accident. Rather, we were introduced to a book entitled *"The Contented Baby"* written by a rather stern British nanny. My sister-in-law successfully used the rather rigid methods outlined in the book and swore by its results. The regimen required to effectively sleep-train your infant earned the author the nickname the "Nazi Nanny." For this system to work, we had to meticulously schedule naps, bedtimes and even wake times for our baby in the morning. When grandparents babysat, we got astounded looks when we instructed them to wake up baby from her morning nap after forty-five minutes. "You actually wake the baby from a nap?" That was certainly a foreign concept, but it was crucial in ensuring that the sleep-hungry infant wasn't getting too much shuteye during the day or else that very important 7 p.m. bedtime would be jeopardized. It would also seriously threaten their ability to sleep through the entire night.

If you have kids, you know just how golden it is to be able to put your baby down at 7:00 p.m. and not have to worry until 7:00 the following morning. Like I said, it saved our sanity, especially after a particularly long day of explosive crying. But, getting to the point where your baby will comply with the Nazi Nanny's regimen takes some tough love. That's where our experience with colicky kids came in very handy. Imagine having what some people would describe as an "easy baby." We've all seen those happy, cooing cutie-pies bouncing up and down for hours on end, charming everyone in the room with their toothless grin. Now, imagine putting that bundle of joy down in a crib, closing the door and listening to him cry for fifteen minutes straight! It's enough to break your heart, right? How could anyone with a conscience put an innocent creature through that torturous process?

This very question reminded me of an episode of the 90s sitcom *"Mad About You"* (now I'm really dating myself), where Helen Hunt and Paul Reiser were standing outside their baby's nursery door, debating the merits of letting their daughter cry herself to sleep. Mom was adamant that they needed to let it play out, while Dad was pressing to bust the door down and rock that poor baby to sleep! Lianne and I never once had that debate as we were completely desensitized to the excessive bawling that emanated from our children. We had very little sympathy for their earsplitting protests to being forced into an unwanted nap. They were already crying on and off all damn day, so what was the harm of letting them "self-sooth" for another fifteen minutes?

There were times when Lianne would put baby down and then grab a shower. Problem solved. There were times when I would put Abby down for a nap and go into the basement to exercise on the elliptical trainer. I'd turn on the baby monitor when I got down there and SCREAMING blasted through it. I'd quickly turn it off, start my workout and check again in five minutes. More

SCREAMING! I'd turn it off again and keep working out. Finally, I'd check again after ten minutes and there would be sweet, sweet silence.

Any parent who never had to endure colicky kids may think our sleep-training methods were a bit harsh. But, don't you worry; it didn't last very long and, in the end, it was totally worth it. To this day, our kids still go to bed relatively early, never have an issue going to sleep when we ask them to and have never slept in our bedroom except for those rare times when they had a bad dream. Having adult time to unwind in the evening and a king-sized bed with ample room to spread out for an entire night's sleep is highly recommended, and it all stemmed from a few weeks of tough love.

I'd call that particular parenting strategy a hit, but there have been several misses when it comes to my child-rearing abilities. Discipline is something that can be debated endlessly as everyone has their own methods and theories. I don't claim to have all of the answers, but I do know what doesn't work for us. At the very top of my list is yelling, a behavior that is so ingrained into my parenting that I still find myself shouting at the top of my lungs far too often, even though I know it just doesn't work.

It started very early in the process and just never stopped. The first time I yelled at Abby was after a long morning of fussiness and crying on her part. She was screaming as I changed her diaper. She was screaming as I changed her into clean PJs. She was screaming as I tried to put her down for a nap. Finally, I snapped. I leaned into the crib and roared "SHUT UP!" right into her puffy, beet-red, tear-stained face. For a split second, her eyes popped wide open. She seemed startled, as she looked right at me. She had stopped crying, but before I could even finish silently asking myself, "Did that actually work?" she started up again, even louder than before.

It wasn't my proudest parenting moment. While I didn't make a habit of screaming into cribs, I did continue to yell at my kids at various stages of their development, guaranteeing that they would also learn how to yell at each other and, ultimately, me. For a while, it seemed my kids would actually tune me out when my volume increased which was a sure sign I had reached a saturation point. I would yell and get no reaction; but if Lianne yelled at them just moments later, the kids would stop whatever they were doing and see what she was so angry about. Mommy yelling at the top of her lungs was a rare occurrence, so they figured that they'd better pay attention. I'm really trying to undo the damage I've done with my excessive yelling, but there are times when I do fall off the wagon. My wife has listened to a couple of parenting audio books while commuting to and from the office and gave me some much-needed pro-tips on how to encourage a calmer dialogue with our children. I have to give her credit where credit is due. I can be ready to blow the lid off our house, but then Lianne can usually swoop in and disarm the bomb and send us all on a path to family harmony. If I can emulate her parenting strategies just little bit more each day, I think I can get there. Let's just say it's a work in progress, but I truly am getting better at putting my rage in a cage.

I recall taking a very different approach with Abby when she was repeatedly getting into trouble at her preschool. I would get pulled aside at pick-up time by her teacher almost daily and get the lowdown on how my little girl sometimes needed multiple timeouts for throwing temper tantrums. For once, I actually realized that my yelling at her wasn't working at all. What I did to try and correct her unacceptable behavior at preschool actually worked wonders (at least for a while), and I was applauded by the teacher for helping Abby really turn the corner on her classroom conduct.

I warned my strong-willed muffin that if she didn't behave herself in school and start showing some self-restraint, she would be getting very long timeouts in her bedroom at home. Like many rooms occupied by little girls, Abby's was a treasure trove of toys, stuffed animals and games. That may prompt you to ask how thirty minutes in that room could be any kind of real punishment. The answer was simple. I stripped that room of absolutely everything that had anything resembling entertainment value. Toys, books, knickknacks - you name it. If she could play with it, it was gone. I remember Abby's face drop when I opened the door to her room to reveal what looked like a prison cell. She had a bed, night table and dresser. That was it. I even removed her stand-up mirror because I knew she enjoyed admiring her own reflection. After slowly turning around to assess the transformation before her, Abby responded, "At least you left my ballerina pictures on the wall." I cheerily replied, "Oops! Thanks for the reminder!" I then pulled them off the wall and walked out of the room, leaving Abby to a very boring timeout in cell block D.

The next day, Abby was the best-behaved kid in her class, and I was temporarily hailed a hero! But, ultimately, that particular form of punishment was difficult to sustain, and it was not a long-term solution. As long as Abby avoided meltdowns and timeouts at school, I would reinstate her cherished belongings and her room would go back to normal. However, I found that I became too lazy to dismantle and then reassemble all of her stuff every time she misbehaved and then served her time. It was a clever social experiment and a funny story to tell other parents at parties - but not very practical.

One of my biggest fears as the primary caregiver is how my parenting decisions are shaping my kids. When I first took this gig, I honestly thought that I would have much more patience; but I find that those crazy kids have me wound up pretty tight most of the time. Lianne once told me that she was very surprised how quickly I could lose my patience and fly off the handle since it was extremely rare to see my temper flare prior to becoming a father. Before I left my job, my co-workers would assure me that because I was so laid back, I was sure to be a cool dad. You know what? I actually believed them, so even I am occasionally shocked to see my transformation from the mild-mannered Bruce Banner into HULK SMASH!

I remember a rerun of *The Simpsons* where Bart writes a comic book called "Angry Dad," and the first thing I thought was, "Is that how I'm seen in our household?" Because the kids spend the most time with me, I'm the one who usually has to be the disciplinarian. It's not fun to always play the heavy, so sometimes I wait until Lianne comes home before punishments are doled out.

It's a 21st century twist on the classic line "You just wait until your father comes home!" I try not to make a habit of doing that as it's really not fair to my wife. Sometimes, Lianne doesn't even come home from work until the kids are almost ready for bed, so I'm positive she doesn't want to be the bad guy the second she walks through the door. But, there are days when I just don't have the mental fortitude to deal with the latest unfortunate incident that left either one or both of my children in tears, and I end up punting the ball.

Now, don't be under the impression that my life at home has turned me into a school principal whose only job it is to deal with a non-stop parade of bad behavior and administer disciplinary actions. I believe my kids see me as bad cop and good cop as we've had infinitely more good days than bad. And, for the most part, I've been blessed with two pretty good eggs.

Knowing Abby and Daniel are starting off their lives as fairly decent human beings, I still worry about who my kids are becoming as they race toward their tweens, then teens and finally adulthood. Do they do enough around the house? Are they spoiled? How do they treat their friends? Do they respect their elders enough? How are their manners? There are times when I complain about my kids' bad habits to other parents, and I usually get the same response: "What are you talking about? Your kids are great!" I'll admit that when we have company over, our children seem to really step up their game and exhibit pleasant behavior and surprisingly good manners. They've even been known to clear the dinner dishes without being prompted. My response to these houseguests is always the same: "What you've just witnessed is not an accurate depiction of my children."

Am I being hard on myself? Am I not being hard enough on my kids? Over a decade as a stay-at-home dad and it's still very easy to second-guess myself. With the exception of our cherished kidless getaways, I've been watching over my brood every day of their lives. When they were younger, it was all day, every day. Even though they are both school age now, I'm still the one picking them up from school, driving them around the city for music, gymnastics and soccer, and then making (or buying) them dinner. I sometimes wonder how different their personalities would be if I were the one bringing home copious amounts of bacon and Lianne were the stay-at-home parent. I really don't know, but something tells me they wouldn't be nearly as loud and annoying.

I truly believe that a person's character is hardwired from birth, but I still fear that if my offspring end up as a couple of duds it's on me.

I'll be forced to put my head down, raise my right hand over my head and blurt out, "My bad." I know that it takes a village, but if society labels your kids as "bad apples," the list of people to blame is usually pretty short. Have I made mistakes? Absolutely. Everybody does, and making huge missteps in the working world can often have serious consequences on one's career trajectory, earning potential and personal growth.

If my tenure as primary caregiver is riddled with one terrible mistake after another, the cost can't be measured in any currency, but rather in the development of young human beings. There have been times when I thought that the stakes weren't really all that high in what I do for a living, but in many ways they could not be higher. But, here's the good news. I'm really only halfway through the first phase of parenting. I now have over ten years of experience under my belt, but I still have another full decade to go before I can finally claim that I helped guide two precious humans from helpless infants to independent adults.

I obviously have a very long way to go, so there's still plenty of time to either right this ship or completely sink it. The next few years will see both Abby and Daniel enter their teens, and I'm not sure I'm looking forward to navigating through that potential shitstorm. For now, I'm thankful that simply taking away their iPad minis, Nintendo DSs and coveted computer time has proven to be the most successful disciplinary tools yet. How much longer that will work remains to be seen, but I must say it has definitely decreased my penchant to yell first and ask questions later.

WHEN OTHER PEOPLE'S KIDS
ARE THE IDIOTS

It's obvious I have a hard enough time trying to control or modify the behaviour of my two kids. Any parent can relate to this daily struggle. As primary caregiver, I feel that I have had the biggest influence on the development of the little hooligans who live in my house, and that scares me... a lot!

I place a lot of importance on how my offspring behave in public, as I firmly believe how people represent themselves to the world at large says a lot about their character, and directly correlates to how successful they will be later in life. (This obviously doesn't apply to the Donald Trumps of the world, but I digress.) The demeanour my kids have displayed in public has ranged from surprisingly exemplary to downright embarrassing, but I do my best to try and keep them in line.

Like I said, it's pretty difficult to keep my own kids from behaving like animals, but what about other people's kids? Do we have a right to discipline, or "set someone straight" if witnessing inappropriate behavior from a smaller person who does not share your DNA? There's a bit of grey area here, but if I had to make a definitive call, I'd would say: YES, all parents have a responsibility to point out and try to correct poor choices and bad behaviour in other people's kids.

Being a stay-at-home Dad has meant that I have been exposed to children... a LOT of children. Too many children! GAHHH! Get these children away from me! I've been to every playground in a five kilometre radius of my house, I've volunteered at almost every school field trip for ten years running, I've coached soccer and basketball teams and I've helped host countless birthday parties and sleepovers.

Big kids, small kids, fat kids, skinny kids, happy kids, whiny kids, smart kids, dumb kids, clean kids, dirty kids, my kids, your kids. Trust me, I've seen them all and the one thing I can tell you with absolute certainty: I have zero tolerance for idiots.

Is it just me, or does it seem like most kids these days are uncontrollable maniacs? Growing up in the 70's meant that corporal punishment was still allowed in schools. I remember vividly watching classmates get "the strap"- a long, thick leather strip that was kept in the top drawer of the principal's desk drawer. Trust me, witnessing that instrument of instant pain kept me on the straight and narrow path at school. I also remember seeing other parents discipline kids that weren't their own, even spank them! Times certainly have changed, and while I certainly don't advocate whipping kids with leather straps or doling out bare-bum spanks to strangers, I will step in and give a kid a piece of my mind if they are acting like an idiot.

One incident that stands out happened when Abby was barely out of toddlerhood. She was maybe four-years-old and we were at the zoo, which has a massive playground with multiple climbing structures designed for various age groups. After spending some time with the other younglings in the "ages 2-5 zone", Abby insisted on playing with the big kids. So, off we went to the "ages 6-11 zone", where she was promptly bowled over by some stocky eight-year-old with a head of steam and zero cares that he had just sent little Abby flying. I immediately rushed over to her to wipe away some tears and make sure she was OK, and then I made a B-line straight towards the young offender. I was enraged:

"Hey! Didn't you see that you just knocked over that little girl? She's only four-years-old and you just ran her over and didn't even stop to say sorry or see if she was OK!!!"

I was on my knees, eye-to-eye, right in his face – yelling at a young boy. His eyes widened, he didn't say anything and he looked frightened. As he ran off, I felt a sudden pang of guilt as I realized that I just scared the bejeezus out of a little kid. I anxiously watched his path as he found his mother and tearfully relayed the story to her. They were actually close enough to me that I could hear the conversation.

"Mommy! This man was just yelling at me and he said I pushed over a girl and he was yelling and he scared me... and... and..."

The mother didn't even bat an eye or get up off the bench as she set down her magazine and interrupted her son, "Did you knock the little girl over?"

"Well, yes", he sheepishly replied.

Without skipping a beat the mother calmly replied, "Then you deserved to be yelled at."

She then crossed her legs, picked up her magazine and turned away from her son. That was it. That was how she handled it. I let out a huge sigh, relieved the incident was over and thought to myself: "I'm glad she gets it". I was fully prepared to engage in what could have been a heated debate about disciplining other people's kids, but there was no need for confrontation. She was a parent who understood that her son had acted like an idiot and was called out for it.

Another playground incident comes to mind, but this one didn't end with the same feeling that juvenile justice had been served. I was at Daniel's school when he was about five or six-years-old, and I was volunteering as a playground monitor. Well, one day I was getting all manner of complaints about a certain idiot boy who was at the top of the slide and not moving. He was simply blocking it at the top causing a massive traffic jam behind him. The complaints from the throng of kids piled up at his rear end were having zero effect on his obstructionist stance. I politely asked him to move along, but all he did was glare at me with angry eyes.

And then he yelled back at me, "You're not my Dad! I don't have to listen to you!"

I was momentarily stunned. This kid was maybe five-years-old and he basically just told an adult to go fuck himself. I found this lack of respect staggering, but I calmly responded that he could either slide down or I would find a teacher. I was reduced to my only option... "Move it, or I'm gonna tell on you!" But it worked.

The incident made me think about how this kid, this idiot, came to the conclusion that treating adults with utter disdain was OK. Did his parents instill this unfortunate value system? Did his parents even care? I'm pretty sure if this was the kid who bowled over Abby a few years earlier, I would have had a very different situation on my hands.

Another issue up for debate is how you can treat kids that you are charged with supervising. Must you always be pleasant and respectful of their delicate feelings at all times? Not on my watch! I recall a field trip to an agricultural exhibition where I was "gifted" five first grade boys to watch for the day. Trying to wrangle this band of idiots, (my son being one of them), was one of the most trying days of my life. They would not listen to a word I said, they ran away from me, they ran into people, they all discovered the rope-braiding station and proceeded to whip each other as hard as they could with 4-foot ropes. At the start of the day, I was lecturing them in relatively dulcet tones about appropriate behaviour in public. By the end of the day, I was constantly screaming at these hooligans to stop acting like animals! I felt no remorse for yelling at kids who weren't my own, as I stuck to my personal policy of calling out idiots.

I would like to think that as kids get older, they would mature… even just a little bit. Think again. For Daniel's birthday, we invited six of

Daniel's friends for a sleepover. My son had assured me that he had invited some of the "calmer" boys in his class. If these guys were the more sedate crew, I would hate to see the crazy ones. We tried to confine the carnage in the basement, but the entire house was shaking. The noise... oh dear God, the noise! We've hosted a few girl sleepovers, but nothing compares to boys and the havoc they can create.

As the night wore on, us grown-ups locked up the house, turned on the alarm system and tried to go to sleep. The noise didn't stop. In fact, it got so loud that the boys triggered the alarm system, which is designed to go off when it hears the sound of glass shattering. No glass was shattered, but eardrums may have been. The bedside clock glowed at 2:13 A.M. Finally, enough was enough. Once again, the time had come for me to set some idiots straight. I went down into the basement, the heart of the beast, and laid down the law. There was a bit of yelling, but mostly pleading at this point. Once again, there were different reactions to my bold proclamation. Most of the boys looked at me with sheepish, wide eyes but a couple of them gave me at look that could only be translated as "whatever". At that point of the evening, I was too tired to be offended, and I certainly didn't have the energy to lecture anyone about respecting their elders... I just wanted them to be quiet. And thankfully, the earthquakes stopped and our suffering ended.

I found out the next day that my son took charge of the situation after I retreated upstairs. He managed to keep the boys in check and proved that being an idiot is something that you can potentially grow out of! He actually listened to what a grown-up had to say and behaved accordingly. Imagine that. What's even more impressive is that his friends followed suit.

Is there hope that my days of patrolling and controlling idiotic behaviour are finally coming to an end? Or will my children simply graduate to some kind of next-level idiocy that comes with a completely different set of problems? Time will tell. For now, I must remain vigilant and keep hoping that model behavior from my kids, and all kids... all over the world, is just around the corner.

A man can dream.

STORY TIME

I really wish that I had been writing down some of the more memorable moments that I've experienced while out in the world with my kids. There have been times when I've laughed, cried, almost died from embarrassment and nearly lost my mind from sheer panic. I know there are dozens of stories that are worthy, but Lord help me, I can only remember a few of them as I reflect on ten years as a stay-at-home dad.

Anyone who has had a kid within the last decade knows about *Dora the Explorer*. Once little Abby saw that cartoon, she was hooked on it and could watch it repeatedly. Dora speaks both English and Spanish, and I didn't realize how much our smart toddler was picking up from the adventures of a little girl and her monkey sidekick "Boots." I would soon find out. Just half a block from our house, we were lucky enough to have a playground and Abby was finally big enough to really enjoy it and build up some confidence by crawling all over the various play structures. Normally, I would help her to the top of the slide, but on this day she was adamant that she climb up the ladder all by herself. When she got to the top, she just stood there, frozen. I was sitting on the park bench, only half paying attention when I heard her yell out something that sounded like "you da man!"

"You da man?" I was looking at her, wondering where she heard that kind of slang; and she kept on yelling it, each time a little louder, each time with more urgency - "You da man! You da man! You da man!" Still confused, I yelled back, "Abby, what do you want? Why am I the man?" And then it hit me as I could hear increased panic in her voice. She was too scared to slide down by herself and was pleading for help, but in Spanish, **"¡Ayúdeme! ¡Ayúdeme! ¡Ayúdeme!"** I rushed over and helped her down, but not before receiving a stern talking to from my bilingual baby. "Why didn't you help me?" asked my Twenty-three-month old daughter. Twenty-three months and she already knew more Spanish than me.

After that major miscommunication, I explained to Abby that if she's really in trouble she should only speak English, as Daddy isn't fluent in Spanish. Just a few weeks later, Abby once again yelled for help, but this time I actually would have preferred that she had yelled in a foreign language! We had been cruising around IKEA for about half an hour, picking up some household items and I was almost ready for a Swedish meatball break at the cafeteria. Abby was in the cart, enjoying her ride around the store, and she had been quiet as a mouse the entire time.

Then it started: "Help! Help! HELP!" she shouted, over and over. I didn't want to look like I was trying to silence her, as that would make me look like a kidnapper, so I politely asked her to whisper, or be just a little bit quieter. "Help! HELP!" she continued to bellow, as I started to get a few sideways glances from other shoppers. There was no stopping her increasingly louder calls for help, so I just smiled at people walking nearby, looking rather sheepish. At least I hoped that I looked sheepish... anything but guilty! Finally, Abby revealed what was behind her urgent request for assistance. "Hurry, Daddy, we've got to help baby bird! She's trapped at the top of Tall Mountain!" Damn that Dora! I recognized that particular scenario from an episode of Abby's newest Dora DVD, *Super Silly Fiesta*. That bilingual explorer with no parental figures was still causing me trouble!

Fortunately, no one reported me to store security and Abby and I did get those meatballs eventually. I don't even hold a grudge against that cartoon girl with the bowl haircut because she actually saved the day about six months prior to the dual "Help!" related incidents. Lianne and I will be forever in her debt, as there was a particular weekend when a nasty stomach bug completely floored both of us. We couldn't stray far from the toilet, as everything was coming up, and with very little warning. Lianne and I were laying on our living room floor, barely moving, barely alive and not capable of handling even the most basic of parenting responsibilities. We had considered calling one of our parents to come and get Abby, as we were both unfit for active duty. However, that drastic action was not required, as once we inserted the first Dora DVD into the player, the marathon didn't stop for several hours, allowing Mommy and Daddy time to recover and get back on their feet. Once again, mindless entertainment saves the day. God bless television.

While it was merely a minor inconvenience when Abby made me look like a child abductor in IKEA, her actions in a bank the following year inflicted catastrophic embarrassment on yours truly. These days, I have very little need to physically visit a bank, but I had recently rolled one year's worth of loose coins and probably had about $85 in pennies, dimes, quarters and so forth. I was carrying baby Daniel in one arm and was holding a rather heavy bag of coins in the other. Abby was at my side tugging on my jacket, desperate to get my attention. We were next in line to see the bank teller, so I was trying to get Abby to quickly tell me whatever she needed to tell me. She was whispering something that I couldn't quite make out, but it sounded like it had something to do with "boots." I asked her to repeat her question as I made my way to the front of the line and started to unload several rolls of coins onto the counter. Again, she was whispering something about boots and I was starting to get frustrated, so I sternly told her "Abby, I can't understand you! You have to speak loud and clear so I know what you are talking about!"

And then it came, clear as a bell and loud enough for most of the bank to hear. "I said, SHE – HAS – BIG – BOOBS!" Oh my God. As I heard the sound of muffled laughter all around me, I glanced over to the teller in the next booth and she just shook her head and kept her head down, trying not to smile. I didn't quite know what to do or where to look next. I couldn't look our big-boobed teller in the eye, and I certainly wasn't going to look anywhere near her "frontal region," so I just looked down at the floor and waited for what seemed like an eternity for the coins to be counted and deposited into our account. I really couldn't be angry with my daughter, because she initially tried to discreetly whisper her astute observation about the teller's breast size. Then she did exactly what I had asked her to do, and that was to speak up and be heard! I think I mumbled a quick thank you before bolting out of the bank, but by the time we got back into the car, the extreme embarrassment had already faded. This was some funny shit, and I couldn't wait to start telling everybody I knew about Abby's very public faux pas.

There would be plenty more awkward moments that I would share with my children, and the next story involves Daniel and his "I won't let Daddy out of my sight" phase. We were on vacation halfway around the world, visiting my brother and his family in Vietnam. Daniel was only a year old, and we seemed to be joined at the hip. I know plenty of moms experience this phenomenon, but this didn't happen with Abby, so it was very new to me. We were staying at a beachside resort in southern Vietnam for a few days, and my boy was acting especially clingy. I remember hanging out with everybody on the pool deck and drinking copious amounts of beer. Then I headed off to the washroom to relieve myself, only to find out that Daniel pitched a fit mere moments after I left and not even Mommy could ease his separation anxiety.

So, for the rest of the afternoon I had a very small chaperone every time I went to the washroom which, after six beers, was turning out to be a fairly regular occurrence. The first time I brought him into the can, I set him down on the floor as I tried to use the urinal. That was a non-starter as Daniel cried and grabbed my leg, begging to be carried. So, I was forced to multi-task. I was standing at the urinal, holding a baby on the left, and something much smaller on the right. It wasn't the smoothest transaction ever, but I was getting the hang of it. Then another guy (German, I think) walks into the bathroom, sees us and laughs, "Now I've seen it all! It looks like you could use an extra hand!" I wasn't sure if he was offering to hold either of my "packages," so I just laughed it off and exited the facility as quickly as I could.

Not every anecdote ends up being funny or embarrassing. This last one was downright scary. I was out with the kids running errands, with my final stop being Shoppers Drug Mart. I can't remember exactly what I was there for, but I do remember holding Daniel in one arm and constantly chasing after Abby who was prone to taking off. I was placing items in my shopping basket and yelling, "Abby, please stay close to Daddy, stay somewhere I can see you!" As I drifted from aisle to aisle, Abby was following my instructions, more or less, but then after a minute or so I noticed that I couldn't see or hear her anymore. I yelled, "Abby, come back here! We're going to the checkout!" Nothing. I yelled again and started walking briskly from aisle to aisle, each time calling out her name. I noticed that a little old lady with a cane was watching this unfold and she started getting very nervous. She struggled to keep up with me, following me up and down the aisles, crying out, "Oh dear! Oh no! Oh dear!" over and over as my search became more frantic. By now, I was running all over the store, calling out her name and still nothing. I still had my elderly companion, who seemed almost as stressed as me, watching my every move.

I was this close to going to the checkout to ask if they could make an announcement over the speaker system when I thought of one more place to look. Off to the side of the pharmacy area, there was a tiny waiting room where they had a few chairs, a blood pressure machine and, best of all, one of those toys with a maze of winding, brightly coloured wires on which you slide wooden beads back and forth. And there she was, quietly playing with the beads, without a care in the world. I could finally breathe again, and I rushed over to Abby to give her a big hug and then a firm reprimand for wandering off and scaring the life out of me. The little old lady gave me a big smile, exhaled loudly and said, "Oh, thank heavens!"

As she made her way out of the store, I squeezed Abby's hand and went to the checkout line. It's amazing how quickly sheer panic can give way to a warm wave of overwhelming relief. "Daddy, let go of my hand!" Abby was already trying to squirm out of my grasp, but this time I wasn't about to let her go ... at least not until my heart rate slowed back down.

WHAT ARE YOU GOING TO DO
WITH ALL OF THAT FREE TIME?

I've heard that phrase quite a few times over the years and, while some homemakers take great offense to that particular question, I've always taken it in stride. The fact is, the amount of "me time" allotted to yours truly has varied greatly over the past twelve years, ranging from practically zero to "Hey, I have time to write a book!" When I first began this journey into a fully domesticated life, Abby was just six months old. By the time my first shift at home started, she was napping two or three times a day, with the afternoon siesta lasting almost an hour and a half. As I've already pointed out, our baby girl could be demanding and sometimes completely exhausting, so I wanted to make the downtime count. You probably assumed that sitting on my fat ass would be my number one priority, but it was that very fat ass that prodded me into a more product-ive use of Abby's afternoon slumber.

A few months before I quit my job, I took a solo trip to my grandmother's ninetieth birthday celebration. I'm telling you this because when I saw myself in the family photo of all of the rela-tives who made the trip for the party, my eyes neared popped out of their sockets. Good Lord! How did I get so freakin' fat? There I was, stand-ing in the back row with a military-style buzz-cut, wearing a huge wool sweater, the spitting image of John Candy in the movie *Stripes*. When I first met Lianne, I was around 185 pounds, but seven years of marriage had not been kind to my waist-line and I was tipping the scales at 230 pounds. I knew I would spend my downtime shedding as much weight as humanly possible.

We already had an elliptical trainer set up in the basement, but I needed more equipment to try and melt away the massive spare tire that had circled my torso. I can't remember what it was called … the Ab-Blaster? Abdominator? Ab-Roller? Whatever it was, it was a mechanism that helped perform crunches and isolate the abs! Did it work? Actually, nothing really worked at first, so I started another phase in my weight loss regime … SlimFast. I bought it by the case and faithfully drank a can for breakfast, another for lunch, and then had a sensible dinner. That was the company catch phrase, so I stuck to the regimen and started to see some slimming, but it wasn't exactly fast.

I needed to add another element, but this one I still regret to this day because I'm pretty sure it wasn't the healthiest solution. Diet pills! I made my way to the "Health Food" store at the mall and bought a giant bottle of these little white pills that promised to melt the pounds away. After reading the list of active ingredients, it was obvious that I was about to bombard by body with several different caffeine derivatives. All the pills really did was keep your heart beating like a jackhammer, fooling your body into thinking it was actually exercising, but burning calories nonetheless. I was supposed to take three pills a day, but I soon realized that the evening pill would give me such a jolt to my system that I couldn't even close my eyes at bedtime. So I reduced my dose to only two pills, but even that didn't sit well with me. It was a strange feeling to be leisurely laying on the floor, watching a video with Abby, and periodically checking my pulse to find that it was still racing like I had just finished running a marathon.

Despite my reservations, I stayed on the pills because of one simple fact - I was dropping pounds like gangbusters. Yet, somehow, this three-pronged effort of exercise, SlimFast and excessive caffeine intake still wasn't enough. I needed a fourth prong, something more to get me over that hump. So I adopted an age-old trick used by teenaged girls to try and curb their appetite. I started smoking! I'd been a smoker on and off since my late teens, but was never what you would call a heavy smoker. My peak daily cigarette total never even reached double digits, and by the time I met Lianne I was down to one or two a day. I had quit completely a couple of years after we got married, but I couldn't think of a better time to restart that filthy habit than during my "Let's get healthy" phase. Looking back, I still can't believe I put my body through this process, but, when something is working, sometimes you can't see the forest for the trees.

To recap, I had shed pounds like nobody's business, but I can't say I would ever recommend this method where I drank hundreds of cans of a weight-loss mixture chock-full of good stuff like maltodextrin, potassium phosphate and carboxymethyl cellulose. I topped it off with pills that made me feel wired all day, and the icing on the cake was three or four evening smokes to take the edge off. I justified this truly terrible regimen by reminding myself that I was still exercising almost daily, so maybe that evened it all out. After almost a full year of this madness, I had reached my target weight of 180 pounds. I had lost 50 pounds! The immediate effects were apparent when I put on my baggy wardrobe every day, but did the weight loss actually change the way I conducted my day-to-day routine as a stay-at-home dad? It did in one measurable way, and that was with my energy level. I found the endless trips lugging my self up and down the stairs in our home increasingly less taxing. Imagine carrying a fifty-pound sack of flour up and down a flight of stairs fifty times a day – that was me at 230 pounds. I was practically bounding up and down that stairway at 180 pounds.

I looked a whole lot better and enjoyed the compliments of people who hadn't seen me in a while, but ultimately that weight was not sustainable. I didn't want to stay on the pills or the Slim-Fast forever, and I did manage to stop smoking (although I still have cravings!). I was lucky that Abby was still a baby and didn't have to witness her Dad become a pill-popping smoker to "get fit". As for Lianne, I knew that she wasn't a big fan of my unhealthy fat-shedding practices and during my year of rapid weight loss she gently, and repeatedly, encouraged me to try a healthier approach. When we met, I was still a smoker and I appreciated her efforts in getting me to quit. Eight years later, she helped me quit again.

What that year of massive weight loss really gave me was a funny story and quick answer when someone asked me what I've been doing with my free time. I would point to my flatter belly and say, "This is what I've been doing."

While my dumb and dangerous diet was my initial "side project," the activity that has kept me the busiest (when not raising children), has been home renovation/building. I've already talked about the need to finish our basement as our family began its initial expansion phase and how that kept the testosterone flowing through my veins. After our second expansion, our home seemed even smaller, so we toyed with the idea of adding a small addition to the back and renovating the entire main floor. In the end, we decided to build a larger house that could accommodate a family that had doubled its human population.

We bought a home that was already at the framing stage, so we still had to pick all of the interior colours, fixtures and finishings. I have to give my wife most, if not all, of the credit for the end result as she has a real eye for detail and picked a great combination of woodwork, flooring and granite. My contribution was going to the construction site to keep tabs on the construction progress. I have to admit, this particular house build was actually very smooth, and I wasn't catching many glaring errors. I do recall having to reschedule our concrete pour in the backyard as they had prepped the patio five feet too short! For the most part, my daily visits to the job site were stress-free and kind of exciting. I was witnessing every aspect of a home build up close and personal, and it turned out to be a very interesting and educational process.

We moved into our new house when Daniel was one and Abby was three. We felt right at home immediately and honestly thought that this could be our forever home. And I think it could have been if only the kids had stopped growing. Daniel's room was a great size for a nursery; but once he graduated to a big-boy bed and real furniture, we knew that it was only a matter of time before he realized that he got totally shafted in the bedroom department. Our house also had a very small mudroom and practically zero storage. So, after almost six years, we were on the move again, this time to our true forever home. They say third time is the charm, and we wanted to make sure this house would be built exactly the way we dreamed it up.

We loved our inner city neighbourhood and managed to find a lot just three blocks from our house. Unlike our previous build, this would be a true custom job, and we had to select everything from the initial design to the smallest of interior details. Since we had experienced the building process just six years prior, we felt like this would be a breeze. What could possibly go wrong? Wow … where do I begin? While the design and selection phase went smoothly enough, it was the construction stage where everything became unraveled. By now, both of the kids were at school full time, so this home build became my entire life for well over a year. Remember, the job site was only three blocks away, so I would drop in three, four, five times a day.

Now, those who work in the trades are probably thinking that a homeowner watching over every detail of the build like an anal-retentive hawk would be the most annoying thing ever. I even had a few guys working on the construction site bark at me, "Hey, don't you have a job you should be at right now?" I would always snap back, "You know what? This is my job!" I could not have cared less if the trades found my constant presence annoying because I was constantly finding huge mistakes. The following is just a small sample of the construction errors I was uncovering: heating ducts in the wrong spots, tiles laid incorrectly, bathroom framed too small, fireplace mantle the wrong size, baseboards painted the wrong colour, staircases installed incorrectly, all three fireplaces framed wrong, office cabinetry stained the wrong colour, basement wall in the wrong place, multiple mirrors cut the wrong sizes and the list could go on. But, I think you get the picture.

We had a site manager who was supposed to catch all of this stuff, and it's possible that he would have eventually noticed the mistakes. However, the extra time it would take to repair and remedy the multiple mishaps would have set us way behind schedule, and even more over budget. I was finding the errors almost as they happened and well before walls had to be ripped up to fix them. It was a very stressful time, but I have to give our builder some credit. Whenever I found a defect, they fixed it to our complete satisfaction, and we actually ended up with a very beautiful home. To be fair, not all of the trades minded me hovering over them. In the weeks and months after we moved in, we had to endure a parade of guys who were there to fix up the items on our deficiency list. More than a few of them said to me, "You know, it kinda seemed like you were the site manager on this job, Ha ha!" These comments did not amuse me at all, as we paid our high-end builder very handsomely to professionally supervise the construction of our dream home. But without my hawkish oversight, the project that started off with such high hopes could have ended as a complete nightmare.

Now that we've been living here for a few years, I almost forget how painful the process really was and we're actually very happy with how it all turned out. As soon as we settled into our new home and the final fixes were completed, the same old question came up again, "What are you going to do with all of that free time?" But, this time, it wasn't someone else enquiring; it was me, and the answer had always been staring me square in the face. I've had the idea of writing a book about my experiences as a stay-at-home dad from the very beginning. In fact, I mentioned it to my vice president of marketing the day I quit my job, and he said that he looked forward to reading it someday. I always thought it was something I would do in phases as my journey progressed, but life kept getting in the way. When the kids were small, I figured there was no way I had the time to sit and write. Those rugrats kept me running after them all day, and I was definitely too worn out to do it in the evenings. When the kids started getting a bit older, I thought maybe I should start writing things down, and I did to a very small extent.

I actually scribbled some quick notes several years ago, outlining the book in a very rough fashion with some possible chapter titles and even some anecdotes in point form. But, that's as far as I got as more life kept getting in the way. When the kids both reached school age, I confidently determined that would be the time when I would finally tell my story, but then we decided to build a new house and that became my pet project for almost two years.

This book only became real when I announced in my annual Christmas letter that I had begun writing it. The fall of 2013 marked the tenth anniversary of my decision to stay home with the kids, and I couldn't think of a better time to begin documenting the rollercoaster ride that has been fatherhood. I dug up the notes I had jotted down so many years ago and found that I could barely read them, but at least it was a start. I started typing, and by Christmas I had enough of a book that I thought I could reveal my ambitious plan. The biggest reason I chose to go public was to force myself to follow through with this thing! Suddenly, it was "out there," and I knew that I actually had to finish it. Had I kept it quiet, it would have been too easy to write ten pages, bail out and simply say, "Meh, this is too hard; there must be something better to do with my free time."

CLOSING UP SHOP

Our family plan was always straightforward and simple. We would go "two and out" regardless of what combination of genders we were delivered. Two boys, two girls, it really didn't matter. Together, we made two beautiful babies and our million-dollar family was more than enough for us to handle.

Besides, it's common knowledge that the world is designed for a family of four. Hotel rooms, vehicles, homes, restaurants, you name it. Having a fifth wheel can be a huge pain in the ass, so why not keep the family unit at a relatively manageable size? While we were both in agreement that we would halt the baby train after two stops, we may have felt differently if we hadn't experienced the slap of a double dose of colic. Lianne once told me that if she could get an ironclad guarantee that the third kid would be easy-peasy during those first six months, she would almost consider making a trilogy.

There's only one surefire way to know that you are truly ready to close up shop and "lock in" the family size for all eternity. And that's the reaction when faced with the possibility of an unplanned pregnancy! I won't bore you with the details, but a couple of years after Daniel was born, there was a brief moment in time when we thought that Lianne could be knocked up again. Oh, the humanity! There was hand wringing, there was nervous pacing, and there was immediate concern. When all was said and done, it was only a small scare, but what the experience does is provide absolute clarity on the matter at hand. Once we got the all clear, an ocean of relief washed over us both. There was never a "you know, I was kind of getting used to the idea" moment. Nope. I think we may have even got drunk to celebrate. When you joyously raise a glass to not being prego, you should take it as a sign that something permanent has to be done. It was time for me to me make an appointment for a minor procedure with major implications.

I started consulting a few of my buddies who'd had the procedure done to scope out the various doctors and venues available to me in the greater Calgary metropolitan area. There was one very intriguing scenario that a doctor in nearby Banff had cooked up for his patients. He called it "Chip and Snip!" Before you had your balls rendered inert, you could beat some balls around a golf course for nine holes. That sounded like a very pleasant way to ease into self-imposed sterilization, but it was the middle of winter when I was looking to git er done and felt that I needed to strike while the iron was hot before I changed my mind. I had settled on a dude with a clinic near our house. A friend also recommended him, so I don't want you to think my decision to use this particular snipper was based solely on convenience. I'm lazy, but I'm not that lazy.

Before I made the appointment, another friend of mine suggested that I should really get some of my sperm frozen and locked away, just in case. I wasn't sure what scenario would unfold that would require me to father more children, so I was initially unsure about the idea. He clarified that it wasn't about having back-up sperm in case of a divorce and the eventual need to start a second family with wife 2.0. Rather, it was a kind of morbid insurance policy in case anything happened to one or both of our existing kids and we still wanted to have more children while Lianne was still relatively young enough to safely bear them.

I thought about it for a week or so, then decided to take the plunge. Getting a vasectomy and forever crushing my ability to seed the garden seemed so permanent, so I liked the idea of my wiggly sperm living on, at least in suspended animation. It somehow made my decision to go under the knife easier to accept, so I made an appointment at a sperm bank near the University, and agreed to a minimum forty-eight hour state of celibacy before the big day. I guess they wanted me to be as potent as possible before my boys were put on ice.

When I arrived and checked in at reception, I was given a cup and pointed in the direction of a small room at the end of the hall. Once inside, I felt like I was in a scene from a cheesy sitcom. It was everything I thought it would be. A stack of girly magazines on an end table, a couch and a television hanging from the ceiling. There was no ability to change the channel, so I had to endure a porn-parody of the Brady Bunch that was more than a bit off-putting. I know Marsha and Greg weren't biological brother and sister, but the sight of them "together" was weird. The magazine option wasn't any better, as they were seemingly worn out and used up from too much handling. A whole lot of guys had obviously used these tattered publications to get the job done and it showed. The covers were bent, torn and I swear there were a couple of pages near the back of Juggs magazine that were stuck together.

I decided not to touch the magazines and got to the business at hand. In the end, "Marsha! Marsha! Marsha!" took on a new meaning that afternoon. As I strolled back to the reception area with my cup full of mission accomplished, I remembered the words of my buddy who went through this process the previous year. He was adamant that I not simply slink out the door with a sheepish look on my face. Rather, he instructed me to hold my head high, smile and look the receptionist right in the eye when I presented my sample. "You've got nothing to be ashamed of!" he said. "You're doing something great for your family and you should be proud of that!" So, I took his good advice and strutted out the door with a spring in my step.

Now that I had my potential legacy sitting in a freezer, it was time to get real. Step one of this process was to secure safe storage of semen. Done. Step two was to have the actual procedure arranged and executed. Like step one, I had some instructions that had to be carried out before I was ready to officially shoot blanks. During my pre-op visit with the doctor, he told me it was my job to shave the scrotum in preparation of my big day. That was no problem, as I enjoy trying new things. He also asked that I bring a pair of "brief-style" underwear that was at least one size too small. I only wore boxers, so I made sure I had a fresh, tight pair of tighty-whiteys on hand. His only other request was that I not drive myself home after the deed was done.

When the day finally arrived, I was a bit nervous, but ready to rock. The whole thing would only take around ninety minutes from check in to departure, so at least it would be relatively quick. Lianne dropped me off around 10:00 a.m. at the clinic, and by 10:30 I was laying flat on my back with no pants on.

My doctor explained to me that he didn't like giving needles down there, and preferred to use only a topical anesthetic to dull the pain. The idea of getting stuck twice in the old ball-sack didn't sit well with me, so I was completely at ease with his preference. Shortly thereafter, he made two small incisions on either "side," and was ready to snip. I was pleasantly surprised after I felt the first one come and go with very little fanfare. All I felt was a little pinch. That's why I could have used a pencil in my mouth for the other side. Yeee-ouch! That one was definitely more than a pinch and felt more like a punch, but thankfully the discomfort passed quickly. After some tidying up, it was time to send me on my way in my super tight underwear. The doc was a firm believer in keeping everything snug as a bug in a rug, and that's why he stuffed a 4-inch stack of gauze strips in my tighty-whiteys. He wanted to make sure my package was extremely secure, and wasn't going anywhere.

He advised me to simply rest on the couch for the entire weekend and resist the urge to get up and resume normal activities. While laying around for hours on end, one could actually feel pretty darn good, but after a couple hours of moving about, a new wave of pain might come out of nowhere and knock you square on your ass. I told my doctor I would have no problem being a lazy lump on a couch, and the only other instructions he left with me were to "clean the pipes" out at least three times a week to ensure the procedure would be a success. He made sure to remind me that this was a task I could do on my very own, as he was tired of husbands demanding their wives provide extra sessions of marital relations, claiming it was "Doctor's orders!" We also had to be careful to use birth control for three months, as I would need to be tested to make sure my sperm count was indeed zero before I started riding bareback.

I joked that I would have to severely cut back my regimen to clean the pipes only three times a week, and without cracking even a small smirk the doctor sent me on my way, a new man … or was it slightly less of a man? Regardless, I walked across the street to Starbucks to order a celebratory latte and wait for Lianne to pick me up. While waiting at the end of the counter for my hot beverage I happened to look down at the floor, but my eyes never reached that far. I almost gasped out loud when I saw this massive bulge protruding from my crotch! That huge stack of gauze in my underwear had made me almost comically well endowed! Luckily, I was wearing a long coat that was immediately buttoned up to protect the public from my vulgar display. I don't know how many people may have witnessed my prominent projection, but I quickly found a seat in the corner and tried to pretend like it hadn't happened.

My recovery was uneventful, my follow up visit with the doctor was normal and after three months, testing did reveal that my sperm count went from millions and millions to a big, fat zero. My baby-making enterprise was officially closed for business and our family would have to remain at its current population of four humans. The only thing left to do was decide how much longer I would leave my swimmers in cryogenic suspension.

It's been over eight years since my vasectomy, and just a few months ago I received my annual letter from the sperm bank asking for another $220 to keep my sample frozen for another twelve months. With both of us in our mid-forties we decided that even in a purely hypothetical world, our child rearing days were behind us. I signed the release form and mailed it in, and with that my boys were discharged from their icy bondage and sent out to pasture, never to fulfill their ultimate destiny. While I had never hoped my frozen sperm would ever be used, it's still a little sad to let them go and think about the fact that I've finally closed that chapter in my life.

PERCEPTIONS

When the kids were younger, they never once questioned our family's configuration. Mommy worked and Daddy stayed at home, and they never noticed or cared that we were very different from almost every other family they knew. As far as they were concerned, our family unit was just like any other. As my years as a stay-at-home dad started to whiz by, it seemed like Abby and Daniel were toddlers one day and ready for their first day of kindergarten the next. Once they were school age, their increased interaction with classmates exposed them to many more households. They started coming home from school chock full of questions. Why was I the parent who was home? Why wasn't it Mommy? Could we switch places so I could be at work, and Mommy could be at home? I would usually get the latter question right after they were punished for deliberate acts of insubordination, and my response was always the same: "If you think Mommy would be any easier on you guys, then think again! You'd be crying for me to come back after a week!" At least that's what I assumed would happen. Maybe Mommy would be infinitely more popular and reduce the parent-yelling quotient by ninety five per cent.

To explain why I was the parent who stays home to take care of them, I decided that I would sit the kids down and give them the entire history of their mom and dad, starting with how we met and ending with both of them being born. About halfway through my spellbinding account of our family's history, I was talking about the time when we moved into our first house and I was working at a TV station … and both of them halted my story in its tracks and almost jumped out of their seats. "WHAT??? You used to actually work at a real job?" They seemed so shocked with the concept that their dad had a life before they both entered this world and commenced their complete and utter dominion over my existence.

Surprisingly, they actually seemed interested in old "war stories" of my past work experiences, and I even showed them some of my old TV news reports that I appeared in or produced. Maybe it was seeing their dear old dad in a brand new light, but they appeared impressed that I used to have a career that didn't involve preparing Kraft mac and cheese and driving them to gymnastics. When they asked if I ever wanted to go back to work someday, I would answer their query with a barrage of questions directed right back at them: "Who would pick you up from school at 3:30? Would you like to go to afterschool care every day until 5:00? Who would drive you to music, soccer and gymnastics after school? Would you like all of your activities to be on Saturdays? Which activities do you want to give up, because we wouldn't be able to do them all?"

I tried to explain that our household functions pretty well because one parent is available to run around all week long, taking care of kids activities, shopping, cooking and all of the other domestic stuff. I also clarified that it just didn't make sense for me to go back to work as we didn't need the extra income and the extra stress of both parents working while trying to juggle the demands of family life at the same time. They seemed satisfied with my explanation, and I hoped that they understood that while most families had dads who worked, it really wasn't so bad to have me around. Overall, I think my kids view the role I play in our family in a fairly positive light. As I've already mentioned, I don't profess to be the perfect homemaker or the perfect father, but if you really want to know how your kids rate your job performance, look no further than the yearly "Father's Day" school art project.

A couple of years ago, Daniel brought home this carefully painted clay plate which showed all of Dad's varied interests. Each pursuit was depicted by a small clay feature that was molded to look like one of my favourite pastimes and then stuck to the plate. Most of the formed features were instantly recognizable. There was a note showcasing my musical talents and also a football and a golf club recognizing my love of those particular sports. But, I wasn't sure what the square box was at the top of the plate or the weird brown object on the side. It turns out my son thinks I spend too much time surfing the Internet and drinking alcohol. The square box was a computer screen and the other mystery object was actually a bottle of beer. I laughed out loud when he filled me in, and the first thing I said was, "You really do know your dad!"

Just this past year, my daughter brought home a poem that she wrote for a school assignment. It was a composition that takes the first letter of your name to start each line of prose.

DADDY

Determined to try to get us to school on time.
Always is intense when it comes to sports, but
Does not take life too seriously.
Describes himself as silly and funny.
Yells at us only when he thinks it's necessary.

Again, one of my kids nails it right on the head! From what I can glean from school projects, I'd say that I'm doing all right. I think the most important life lessons that I'm trying to pass along to my kids are that they enjoy life and be their own person. I've seen too many children who are already very stressed out by their own existence at a very young age. I'm hoping my mostly easy-going attitude rubs off on my offspring because life is too short to feel overwhelmed by the age of ten.

I think I have a pretty good handle on how my kids perceive me, but reading other people is not always so cut and dry. I have been very fortunate that both my and Lianne's parents have been nothing but supportive of my decision to leave the workforce and enter the homefront. I was a bit nervous about how my in-laws would react as they probably didn't count on their daughter getting married, starting a family and ending up being the sole breadwinner. That's simply not a family structure that was prevalent in their generation, but thankfully I've never felt it was ever an issue for them.

My siblings have also been encouraging during my journey into domestic life, but at times I feel they think my decision to stay at home has somehow sacrificed my potential for personal success. Maybe it's all in my head, but now and then I also get the odd vibe from certain people that maybe I've "lucked out" into a very financially comfortable life without having put in any of the hard work to get there. It's true that my wife makes a very good living, but I also toiled away as a working stiff for over a decade before packing it all in. When we first got engaged, Lianne's salary was maybe $10,000 more a year than mine was, but it quickly escalated in the years that followed. It was that exponential increase that sealed my fate when we first started to talk about having kids and who would stay at home to raise them.

The fact that I haven't cashed a paycheque in well over a decade doesn't bother me anymore, but I do worry about my wife and the burden that comes with being the only one bringing home the bacon. Right now, our continued livelihood is all riding on the fact that she makes a very good living as a corporate securities lawyer. She's been shouldering the entire responsibility of keeping this family afloat financially for over a decade, and I sometimes wonder if she has any regrets. If she loses her job, there's no way I could ever replace that income. She's locked in … with no way out! Lianne's job can be very high-stress at times, and I've heard more than once that she'd love to switch spots with me, but I'm not sure I really believe her. In any event, that's simply not an option because she hitched her wagon to yours truly. Had she married another lawyer, a doctor or an investment banker, maybe she could have been the one who wound down her career and drove the kids to soccer practice. Oh well. She's 100 per cent stuck with me now; and unless this book sells 15 million copies, she will be until the end of time.

However, whenever I'm feeling particularly financially useless or powerless, I think about an article that I read about successful women with children. Many of them reached lofty heights in their respective fields because they had a husband at home who did the lion's share of the child rearing and domestic duties. So, there you have it, I do have a larger purpose. Behind every great woman there's a man, in an apron. I've made that joke a few times, and it never fails to get a good chuckle.

But, let's take a serious look at my bold statement. That's obviously not the case with every successful woman with kids, as many don't have the luxury of a supportive partner. However, I'm convinced that having a husband take care of the homefront can really make a huge difference in a woman's career trajectory. In 2013, The New York Times published a feature called *Wall Street Mothers, Stay-Home Fathers.* The piece told the story about how several women in the male-dominated field of investment banking were reaping the benefits of having a husband at home by "avoiding domestic distractions" and competing better against other bankers, many of them with stay-at-home wives. It also showed that being the breadwinner often means being taken more seriously in the workplace. One woman interviewing at a big private equity firm explained that her prospective employers actually seemed pleased that her husband stayed-at-home and handled more parenting duties. "It dawned on her that the presumption men had often benefitted from – that they would not be diverted by household demands – was finally applying to her too."

Speaking of women succeeding in life, I came across another interesting piece about the benefits of dads doing a significant amount of household chores. A 2014 article in the Globe and Mail talked about a new gender role study from the University of British Columbia that suggests girls who see their fathers perform domestic tasks become more ambitious and pursue gender-neutral and often higher paying careers. The study showed that homes where dads pitched in even a little, daughters had broader career aspirations, while homes where dads skipped out on household chores saw daughters who were more likely to see themselves as stay-at-home moms. You see? My being a stay-at-home dad is empowering not one, but two generations of women in the very same household! You might be asking yourself: "what about the effect on boys?" The researchers found that it didn't really matter what parental behaviours and attitudes the sons witnessed. Boys chose traditionally male jobs – policemen, firemen, as well as more ambitious professions like doctors and lawyers and such. I guess the old saying could be true: boys will be boys.

As for how the rest of the world sees me, I may have started out as more sensitive to the opinions of others, but now I really don't care all that much. Earlier in this book, I wrote about benefitting from some of the double standards I faced, but this time I'm getting the short end of the stick. While gender roles are always evolving in western society, there's still a very sizable portion of our citizenry that would never dream of criticizing a woman for failing to provide any sort of financial assistance to the family unit. In fact, there are still a surprising number of people who think that all women should be at home taking care of their family's every domestic need. Those same people would also think that a man filling that role would be an abomination.

If I were completely insecure, I would probably overcompensate by promoting my manly attributes or, perhaps go the other way, by pumping up my "stay-at-home cred" on Facebook, looking for validation. But, that's just not me. I know that my family, close friends and pretty much most of civilized society accept my choice to stay home with the kids. And if they don't, that's their prerogative. I've never been a person who worries too much about what other people think of me, and that's served me pretty well as I continue to slog through the swamplands of stay-at-home fatherhood.

I'VE LEARNED

When I started writing this book, I was a couple of months into my tenth year at home. It felt like the right time to celebrate that milestone and finally record my personal history. I had been thinking about (and putting off) starting this little pet project for years, but enough time had finally passed to really show how I've grown into this job, and it has completely changed how I perceive my role as a husband and a father. As I write this, I am now entering my eleventh year in domestic servitude and my self-imposed one-year deadline for finishing this masterpiece is fast approaching.

The process has been an interesting one. I found that days, weeks and even months (especially during summer break) could go by without a single word being written. Other times, I was furiously tapping in notes into my iPhone while waiting in line at Costco, then emailing them back to myself so I wouldn't forget some "bril-liant" thought that sprung into my head.

Clearing out the cobwebs and prying funny anecdotes out of my brain and onto the page was the easy part. Articulating my many stay-at-home-dad adventures and the varied inter-actions I have experienced was simply a matter of organizing them in a semi-linear fashion and typing them out. Once I really got rolling, I didn't find that exercise was all that taxing on the old noggin. Most of it was simply strolling down memory lane and plucking out the highlights. I've enjoyed the process immensely as it seems like a lifetime ago since I've done anything relat-ed to my professional training. I was going to say "since I've done anything work-related," but I had to stop myself right in my tracks. After almost twelve years, I think it's safe to say that being our family's primary caregiver is my job. This is my work. It has taken me a long time to realize that and even longer to finally say it out loud.

What I have been struggling with is figuring out how to finish this damn book and somehow make some sense of my time at home. I need a way to put it all into perspective and communicate what I've learned. Writing this book has forced me to look back at what I've accomplished and look forward to what I still need to do. So, I'm going to impart my wisdom and, in the process, enlighten anyone who's desperate to know what makes a typical stay-at-home dad tick. For this exercise, let's assume that I'm actually a typical specimen.

The most important think I've learned is that me deciding to stay home to raise kids and load the dishwasher on a daily basis has made our marriage stronger. Every marriage has it's ups and downs, and in our twenty years together, we've had countless moments of sweetness, laughter, friendship, passion, compromise and of course, the inevitable arguments and bruised egos. Through it all, I keep thinking how our lives would have been so much more complicated if I kept working at my previous job. What if the past twelve years had been a constant struggle for both of us to balance work and home life? Who would have picked up the kids at daycare? How many arguments would we have had over who could take off early from work to drive Abby to soccer? How many weekends would have featured a weekly spat over whose turn it was to fold the laundry? No marriage is perfect, and there is added financial uncertainty and stress with being a single-income family, but I think the arrangement we started when Abby was just a wee baby has been an unqualified success story. It simply works.

My personal situation has made me curious about all of the other marriages out there like mine. Does having dad stay home equal wedded bliss? There isn't a whole lot of research on this topic, but the *Contemporary Family Therapy* study I referenced earlier does have some pertinent information when comes to couples with a stay-at-home parent. The study shows that regardless of which spouse is the primary caregiver, couples report high levels of satisfaction with their marriages. The are several factors that have contributed to this finding – the couples have shared values on how to raise kids, they are content to live on one income, they are mostly satisfied with the division of household labour and child care, and most importantly, they value and respect the work and contributions of their spouse. That last part rings very true in our household, and we both agree that the strength of our relationship is cemented by the fact it is a true partnership.

Without Lianne, our family would fall apart. Without me, our family would fall apart.

Coming in a close second in this exciting list of important things I've learned is that it's actually OK to ask for help once in a while. After all, if you can't ask your life partner for a hand, who can you ask? My ultimate goal as primary caregiver and homemaker was to try to earn my keep and prove my worth. This meant taking care of business at my end and not dragging my busy wife into the mundane chores of housework, laundry and late-night dashes to the convenience store for milk. I mostly succeeded in this regard, but I lacked in culinary skills. For years, I would tell myself that as long as I had food, any food, on the table when my wife came home, it was mission accomplished. Unfortunately for my family, the quality of my daily menu left a lot to be desired. I rarely prepared anything from scratch as the stack of cookbooks we had accumulated over the years sat on a high shelf in the cupboard, tucked far away from the light of day. I was the king of reheating prepared food! I could heat up stuffed chicken breasts, Uncle Ben's flavoured rice, some frozen peas, and ta-da! A meal fit for a king! Watch me dump a bag of frozen meatballs and a jar of tomato sauce into a saucepan, and shazam! Spaghetti and meatball night is born! Did someone say frozen burritos? No? Well, shut your trap because you're getting them anyways.

It's not like I had some master plan to intentionally prepare unhealthy processed food for our kids when I first became a stay-at-home dad. Rather, it somehow morphed into that unfortunate situation over time. When we first introduced solid food to our babies, we were blending our very own nutritious organic concoctions and freezing them into ice cube trays. We'd reheat a couple of cubes and voila! Abby was eating asparagus with chicken and parsnips! Once the kids grew out of eating my mushed up master-pieces, they started turning up their noses at the grown-up food placed before them at the dinner table. I was dismayed, but I failed to keep them on a healthy track. I even attended a "healthy eat-ing for fussy kids" seminar where the instructor explained that it could take fourteen tries before they will ultimately eat a particular food that you are trying to get them to choke down. Four-teen tries? Really? Or they could simply eat Kraft Dinner and chicken strips for the third time this week. Can you guess which path I chose?

The upside to having very little skill in the kitchen is you can sometimes take major short-cuts and get away with it. I remember when the kids were taking a music class and the teacher would invite the parents to a Christmas recital to showcase what the kids had learned. After the performance, we would all partake in a mini-pot-luck of seasonal baking that was brought in by the parents. The other moms brought beautiful homemade treats - and then there was my con-tribution. I found that if I bought a jumbo pack of individually wrapped Rice Krispie squares, removed that pesky packaging and stacked them into a tupperware container, it kinda-sorta looked like I actually made them myself. I would always feel guilty as the kids would line up for my "baking" while the homemade goodies sat untouched. I've pulled that stunt several times over the years and it never failed to please.

Once in a while, I would make a proper meal and feel pretty good about myself, but that was the exception and not the rule. I just don't love the art of cooking, despite being the head cook of our family operation for over a decade. All of this changed a couple of years ago when Lianne decided that she wanted to eat healthier and try a new low-carb diet that would require all meals to be prepared from scratch. Hey, this sounded like a lot of work for yours truly! As top chef this would be a drastic change to my regular bill of fare, and initially I wasn't ready to embrace this major overhaul in my kitchen.

Despite my reservations, I went along with this bold, new initiative all because I did something that I should have done years ago - ask for help with meal planning. With my wife's guidance, we followed the strict requirements of the diet, and I had never been so busy with dinner prep. There were sauces that needed to be made, roasts that needed to be checked and stirfries that needed to be both stirred and fried. It was a lot of work at first, but so worth it. The official "diet phase" may be over, but the meal planning and recipes remained as a healthy legacy. Who needs frozen meatballs? I now make my own. Did you know that I make pretty great lasagna in a slow cooker? You do now. I've probably handled more fresh meat and vegetables in the past year than I did the previous ten and, while it hasn't transformed me into a master chef, it has transformed me in other ways. The diet and healthy eating that was initiated because my wife wanted to lose a few pounds ended up slimming me down by twenty-five pounds. And do you remember those fussy kids who grew up on Kraft Dinner? Even they love the new menu. Why didn't I ditch the processed food years ago? Oh yeah, because I'm kind of lazy and averse to change.

Lianne usually plans out ten days' worth of meals and gives me a handy-dandy list that includes the name of the cookbook and the page number of the recipe. The grunt work still falls under my jurisdiction as I still have to buy the groceries and make the meals on the weekdays, but having a plan in place that a culinary-deficient specimen like me can easily follow has made all the difference. My weakness turned into one of my greatest strengths all because I was man enough to admit I was a pretty crappy cook who needed some help.

While I do confess to needing assistance on the meal preparation front, I have never asked for help with any of my other domestic duties. And I am happy to report that I've even made some minor progress with my efficiency. Case in point: it's been almost a year since my daughter has had to berate me for allowing her to run out of clean underwear. A small victory to be sure, but I will take it. The bottom line is I'll never be a domestic superstar, but I really don't have to be. I've never actually ironed a shirt as I found out that the drycleaner would launder men's shirts for mere pennies a glass. Sure, women's "blouses" cost about $1,000 per, but that's neither here nor there.

Speaking of being lazy, another thing I've learned is that it's OK to have the odd day where a casual observer would be forced to describe my behaviour as idle, sluggish, lethargic, languid or even slothful. Why do I not feel guilty for not filling each and every day with meaningful tasks to help my family unit run as smoothly as possible? Allow me to enlighten you.

In the fall of 2005, my wife wrapped up her second and final maternity leave, jumped back into the workforce and left me to wrangle a two-year-old toddler and a six-month-old baby. Make no mistake, I still look back at that time and wonder how I made it through some of those days. Those long, long, loooooong days when Lianne left the house early in the morning and was sometimes stuck working late into the evening. I feel that I really earned my keep those first few years of juggling two very young kids and having very little interaction with people my own height. Another very big reason I feel I deserve a bit of downtime once in a while is the number 5,000. That's my estimate of how many dirty, rotten, stinking diapers I've changed in my lifetime. This is a job where you can really get your hands dirty, and I won't soon forget some of the more explosive ass-bombs my kids forced me to clean up. Even if only one per cent of those 5,000 were true diaper disasters, that's still fifty times that sticky baby goop blasted up their backs, completely soiled their freshly washed jumper and ruined my afternoon. I recall one particular poop-splattering incident was so colossal, the only thing I could think to do about it was to take baby Abby with me into the shower and start stripping her down and begin the clean-up process with multiple shower heads helping the cause.

I also usually make time in my daily routine to work out guilt-free because I remember vividly when I had two kids constantly pulling at my pant legs and zero time to exercise. And if I make an extended stop at a coffee shop on the way to get groceries, I remember the days when I couldn't find the time to make a single cuppa joe at home when both kids had terrible colds and were driving me up the wall. When I feel guilty about abandoning my family and golfing Sunday mornings in the summer, I remember the time when Daniel threw up directly into my mouth. I could go on, but you probably get the picture.

Sometimes those lazy days give me pause for thought on the choices I've made since staying home, and even the life-altering decision to leave work and be at home full time. I've learned that once in a while, it's OK to wonder what could have been. What if I decided to stay in my advertising job? Would I have moved on to bigger and better job opportunities? Could I have provided my family with a secondary, but still very significant, income that would have dramatically reduced my wonderful wife's stress level? Maybe my theoretical great-paying job would have given her the opportunity to try other work options that would pay less, but offer a much better work/home balance.

Another hazard of playing the "what could have been" game is comparing myself to successful co-workers and wondering if that could have been me reaching their levels of achievement. However, I never allow all of these brief bleak thoughts to consume me. Life is too short, and I'm quite content with the lifestyle choices that I've made.

I've learned that while there can be a downside to abandoning your career to change 5,000 diapers, there also is a tremendous upside. I'll get to the more mushy, sentimental stuff in a bit, but a very practical advantage to me not working involves vacations. We never have to jump through hoops to coordinate two work schedules with differing amounts of vacation days. When Lianne can take time off, I'm always on call, and always ready to get the hell out of Dodge. We've enjoyed several great family getaways, from Hawaii to California to Vietnam, but nothing will compare to the summer of 2010. That experience practically ensured that my choice to stay at home was the best decision of my life.

Lianne's former law firm allowed their partners to take a three-month paid leave of absence from work every seven years, and she wanted to make damn sure we took full advantage of it. She started planning our adventure almost a year in advance, booking business class flights to France on points, where we would live for the better part of two months. I must say, this trip could only be described as the ultimate pinnacle of our family's happiness. Nothing before it and nothing after it has even come close to replicating that joyous summer.

We started off our trip by renting a place for two weeks on the southern shores of the French Riviera. With our home base in Antibes, we soaked up the sun at the countless beaches in the area and made daytrips to Monaco, Nice,

Cannes and Ile Ste. Marguerite. From the Riviera, we rented a car and worked our way north for a week of sightseeing through Arles, Avignon and Lyon, then settled in a small village in Burgundy for another relaxing two-week stay. This time, the day trips were to wineries! After a few days of exploring castles in the Loire Valley, we finished our French holiday in Paris. There, we rented an apartment for a week and spent very long days pounding the pavement and enjoying the famous sights and sounds of this incredible city. We drenched ourselves in French food, wine and culture. It was simply awesome for the adults, but the kids will tell you their favourite part of our time in France was the final four days spent at Disneyland Paris. Go figure. Even without the visit to Monsieur Mouse, the kids still talk about our European vacation with such fondness. Over six years later and it's become somewhat legendary.

Maybe I'm looking at our trip through wine-coloured glasses, but I honestly can't remember another stretch of time that I've seen my wife so happy, so relaxed and so much fun to be around. The spectacular French vacation notwithstanding, Lianne's entire three-month leave from work was also a major vacation from my life of chores and child rearing as Lianne and I split meals, laundry and anything kid-related. I was in heaven and didn't want it to end. I think the excellent quality family time we shared during this time almost made up for the two colicky maternity leaves that Lianne had to endure when the kids were born ... almost. In any event, I was very pleased that my employment status allowed me to experience this family time. I don't know of many employers that would have allowed me to take two months off work, so I'm very grateful I had the opportunity.

Family vacations are awesome, but something else that we really lucked out with is the ability to go on great trips sans rugrats ... to San Francisco, New York and London. Another very important thing I've learned is that not every stay-at-home parent has it as good as I do. Not by a long shot. With both sets of grandparents living in town, we have been completely spoiled as both grandmas could be considered very hands on. I remember leaving Abby with grandparents for a four-day-long weekend when she was only eight months old! Compare that with some couples who have confided in us that they've never had a weekend away from their kids in six years. Six years? Nope, not since they've been born. Wow. I think our trips without kids really go a long way in keeping our marriage on track and recharging our batteries. Both Lianne's and my parents have to be given a huge thank you for being there for us whenever we needed some alone time. The fringe benefit to all of that time spent with grandparents is that our kids are now very close to all of them.

Now I'll talk about that mushy stuff I briefly alluded to earlier. Feeling this close and connected to my kids is something I would have probably never achieved without my role as the primary caregiver. This is the obvious tremendous upside that I really want to express. I've learned that staying home has made me the "default parent." In other words, I'm the one the kids usually go to first with snack requests, homework problems, bad dreams and skinned knees. That's not at all surprising as I'm the parent who is around them the most, but I didn't know just how deep that connection was and how much the kids counted on my guidance until a semi-humorous, yet awkward incident a couple of years ago.

While washing the kids' laundry, I noticed that Abby's tee shirts were starting to smell a little bit. I was thinking, "Is this body odour? At age ten? Really? When do kids start getting stinky pits?" I mentioned to her that maybe I would buy her some underarm deodorant, and then I explained that in the next couple of years she might notice her body going through other "changes"... the kind that transform a young girl into a ... pubescent girl. I clumsily described the process but added a quick caveat at the end, "But, this is something that you should really talk to your mother about. Trust me on this one." Her response almost floored me. "But, Daddy, why can't I talk to you about this? I would be so embarrassed to talk to Mommy."

I was momentarily stunned and I think I may have nervously chuckled and quipped back, "But, then I might be the one so embarrassed if you talk to me instead of Mommy!" I explained to Abby that her mother had first-hand knowledge of the entire operation, and my daughter seemed placated by this response and didn't seem to notice that I was totally passing the buck. When I retold the story to Lianne, we shared a good laugh, but it reinforced to me how my kids value the role I play in their lives.

At that very moment, I realized that my daughter trusted me implicitly and felt completely free to talk to me about anything … and I mean anything. That felt nice, really nice. Looking back a couple of years later, I wish I had reacted differently. Instead of laughing it off, I should have taken her seriously, assuring her that *of course* she could confide in me. I would have then asked if it was OK if we could let Mommy in on the consultation process and take it from there. That being said, I still think both Abby and Daniel know that they can always come to me and ask me anything … and I mean anything.

Another time that I wish I had responded differently to something one of my kids said involved Daniel, and it stemmed from a fun-filled family conversation that we were having about what the kids wanted to be when they grow up. This particular gabfest took place a few years ago, but writing this book has made me re-examine how I handled it then and how differently I would handle it now.

Abby has told us on numerous occasions that she wants to be a veterinarian when she grows up. She started telling us this when she was four years old and has never once wavered from that position. Daniel, on the other hand, has been all over the map. Over the years, he's mentioned all kinds of professions from firefighter to painter, architect to fashion designer. But, on this day three years ago, my boy told us that when he finished high school he wanted to get married and immediately start a job as a stay-at-home dad. I immediately started laughing and poking holes in his master plan. "First of all," I chuckled, "don't you need at least one kid before you start your new career? Without it, wouldn't that simply make you a househusband without a job?" I specifically remember loudly blurting out, "Dude! Why don't you set your sights a little bit higher?" That got a good laugh from the room and, while I didn't mean to make fun of Daniel, I did try to explain that I went to University for journalism and worked for almost ten years before I became a stay-at-home dad.

Looking back, I don't think that I could have been more clueless. My only son tells me that he wants to be "just like his dad" when he grows up, and I mock him? I know we all thought that my ribbing was all in good fun at the time, but I never stopped for a second to think about why he wanted to be a stay-at-home dad. Did he actually see what I did for a living as something to aspire to? I think my son was trying to tell me that he viewed my "career choice" in a very positive way, and on that fateful day I completely dismissed him and laughed it off.

Maybe I reacted that way because I wasn't truly satisfied then with what I did for a living and didn't want Daniel to think that I was. Since then, I've learned that what I do really is important. The journey I have been on since I began writing this book has released any and all inhibitions and pushed aside all reservations I may have had, compelling me to think about my life at home in a new and different way. There were times when I used to ask myself, "What have I sacrificed by staying home to raise these kids?" When I look at what's really important in this life, I haven't sacrificed a single thing. I've gained more than I will ever know.

In the past twelve years, I have had a front row seat for everything and anything that has even come close to being considered a milestone - first tooth, first words, first wobbly baby steps, first boo-boo, first projectile vomit, first day of school, first eye-roll and more. You name it; I was there for it. I'll still be there for the next round of firsts - first acne break-out, first love, first broken heart, first "I hate you, Dad" - and I swear that I will try to cherish every minute of it all. I've experienced something that very few men ever will, and I'm extremely proud of that.

When our first child was born, so was the idea to author this book. It took me over ten years to finally get off my ass and start writing it. And, by my calculations, we have a little under ten more years before we can punt our second born child out of the house and begin life as empty nesters.

If the next decade of parenthood is as eventful as the first, I'll be in for more life-altering adventures and will accumulate plenty of fresh fodder for my second masterpiece, the inevitable sequel to this first testament of my stay-at-home chronicles. If I were smart and organized, I would start planning by taking notes now of the entertaining episodes that life brings me instead of waiting until the last minute. Oh, who am I kidding? I'll just play it by ear all over again and see what happens. That's how I roll.

And just one more thing.

If my son ever mentions to me again that he wants to be a stay-at-home dad when he grows up, I'll be sure to tell him that nothing in this world would make me prouder.

FINI

AUTHOR BIO

Gregory Tysowski is a certified expert at the stay-at-home dad position. Starting his new gig in the fall of 2003, his career as homemaker really took off in 2005. That's when his responsibilities doubled as he juggled two kids under the age of two, tried to stay on top of the laundry and slow-cooked his way into the rank of top chef. Gregory has been married for over twenty years to his lovely wife, Lianne, and has two children, Abigail and Daniel. Prior to his success on the home front, Gregory received his English degree from the University of Saskatchewan in 1991, and followed that up with a degree in Journalism & Communications from the University of Regina in 1993.

Gregory specialized in Broadcast Journalism, and has worked several jobs in the media business. He started his career as a field producer for a nationally broadcasted CBC news magazine show geared to towards teenagers called "From the Hip". He also worked as a reporter for an educational news program before becoming a writer/producer for a local news outlet. He followed that with a five-year stint in the advertising field, working as an account manager, helping execute the marketing plan for the country's largest sporting goods retailer.

After penning thousands of news stories, a stack of sporting goods catalogues and a dozen installments of his now famous annual Christmas letter – this is Gregory's very first crack at writing a book.

64777930R00110

Made in the USA
Charleston, SC
06 December 2016